WEEK N

PAST TENSE, FUTURE PERFECT

PAST TENSE, FUTURE PERFECT

Successful Management and the Alice Principle

MALCOLM KERRELL

with illustrations by
Ron McTrusty

SOUVENIR PRESS

First published 1996 by
Souvenir Press Ltd,
43 Great Russell Street, London WC1B 3PA
and simultaneously in Canada

ISBN 0 285 63345 7

Typeset by Rowland Phototypesetting Ltd
Bury St Edmunds, Suffolk
Printed by Creative Print & Design Group (Wales), Ebbw Vale

For 'la belle dame aux cheveux blonds',
who encourages me to greater things

ACKNOWLEDGEMENTS

All books are team efforts, not only because of those who have helped directly in their production, but also because of all those many people, now forgotten, who indirectly, and over time, helped to fill the well of knowledge, perception and understanding on which the author draws.

To all those I am grateful, but particular mention must be made of Robin Linnecar, my colleague at KPMG Career Consulting, whose suggestions, help and advice have been invaluable.

Richard Nissen of the Virtual Office Company in London and grandson of the man who invented the Nissen hut, beloved of service men and women in the Second World War, injected some fun into the process of putting the book together by providing the directions, given in the Appendix, for making a genuine Victorian carpenter's hat; he worked out how to do this when faced with the need to find a novel hat for a fancy-dress party . . .

Jenny Martin of Hammicks bookshop in Basingstoke assisted with the bibliography, and Peter Grey of EDC in London helped by giving permission to reproduce the formative and highly relevant matrix model on certainty and agreement used in Chapter 4, a comparison between leadership and management.

Above all Ron McTrusty of the *Evening Standard* has been a good collaborator and friend, providing brilliant and witty illustrations, encapsulating the essence of a character with sharp perception, and giving gentle encouragement when necessary.

I am grateful to the following publishers for giving permission to quote from their publications: Boxtree for the words of one of Scott Adams' 'Dilbert' cartoons; Oxford University Press for quotations from *The Oxford Dictionary of Quotations* and *The Oxford Dictionary of Humorous Quotations*; Routledge for the passage from Rosabeth Moss Kanter's *The Change Masters*; Stainer & Bell for the chorus from Sydney Carter's 'The Lord of the Dance'; Python Productions for the quotation from an episode of *Monty Python's Flying Circus*; Simon & Schuster for the passage from Stephen Covey's *Seven Habits of Highly Effective People*; Pitman for the quotation from Eddie Obeng's *Making Re-engineering Happen*; Arrow Business Books for the extract from Charles Handy's *The Age of Unreason*.

To all these I express my thanks: if you enjoy this book they will share your pleasure and my appreciation.

M. K.

CONTENTS

INTRODUCTION

[Alice] was a little startled by seeing the Cheshire Cat sitting on a bough of a tree a few yards off.

The Cat only grinned when it saw Alice. It looked good-natured, she thought: still it had *very* long claws and a great many teeth, so she felt that it ought to be treated with respect.

'Cheshire Puss,' she began, rather timidly, as she did not at all know whether it would like the name: however, it only grinned a little wider. 'Come, it's pleased so far,' thought Alice, and she went on. 'Would you tell me, please, which way I ought to go from here?'

'That depends a good deal on where you want to get to,' said the Cat.

'I don't much care where—' said Alice.

'Then it doesn't much matter which way you go,' said the Cat.

'—so long as I get *somewhere*,' Alice nodded as an explanation.

'Oh, you're sure to do that,' said the Cat, 'if you only walk long enough.' ... it vanished quite slowly, beginning with the end of the tail, and ending with the grin, which remained some time after the rest of it had gone.

*   *   *

To be employed is to be at risk; to be employable is to be secure

On Tuesday, 11 June, 1996, William Waldegrave addressed the American Chamber of Commerce in London: his subject was job security in the workplace, and he argued that popular concern about this was unjustified, because the average length of time in a job had not decreased significantly over the past twenty years. It was a curious use of statistics—if I am made redundant after being in a job for eighteen years, this may not affect the figures for how long people stay in a job, but it says nothing about how long it will take me to find another one—and ignores totally the number of people (between three-quarters of a million and one million in the United Kingdom at that time) who remain out of work for over a year: *they* know a great deal about job security—or its lack.

In these post-Thatcherite, pre-millennium days, there are many—far too many—people who, confused about the world of work in the future and their place within it, want to know which way they ought to go, without any clear idea of where they want to get to. So they start walking, hopefully but aimlessly, and are then surprised when they find themselves tired, unfulfilled and no further forward in their career search. They may find their own modern version of the Cheshire Cat, but such people by nature tend to talk elliptically, and always seem to vanish at the critical moment . . .

I have spent much of my life helping people get the most out of their career, and most recently, as a career consultant, giving straightforward, practical advice to those who have either lost their job or who want to ensure they don't. Of course nowadays—and probably for as long as our Western culture continues in its present form—there is no surety about any job, and certainly little security of the type William Waldegrave was trying to describe. But there are certain insights, techniques and practices which, combined with wisdom, experience and sheer canniness, may help working men and women to reach that fulfilment in a career which is the apex of Maslow's pyramid. The aim of this book is to make those insights—and men and women—*work*.

I believe the starting-point, the fundamental insight, or premise, is the statement at the start of this Introduction, which I call the Alice Principle: 'To be employed is to be at risk; to be employable is to be secure'—or at least as secure as one can hope to be. If all I have is a job, then I am highly vulnerable, the more so as I get older or out of date with modern developments. If, on the other hand, I have constantly kept abreast of current trends, and possess several marketable, employable *skills*, I can be confident that if I do lose my current job I can transfer those skills to another job without too much difficulty.

This book is designed to show how anyone can move from being employed to being employable; from being, like Alice, indifferent about where we want to get to, to knowing which way we *ought* to go, guided by Alice and the characters she meets.

Two decades ago top business books carried heavy titles like *Spatial Economic Theory* and *The Function and Analysis of Capital Market Rates*. Now *Business Week*'s best-seller list is crammed with volumes with pithy titles like *Leadership Secrets of Attila the Hun, Winnie-the-Pooh on Management* and *Make It So: Leadership Lessons from Star Trek, the Next Generation*. More surprising is the astonishing success of *Jesus C.E.O.: Using Ancient Wisdom for Visionary Leadership*, which sold over 80,000 copies in hardback. Clearly in this soundbite, visual culture, there is a fascination with, and a demand for, books which are concise, entertaining, graphic, memorable and relevant to today's workplace.

There are reasons why the characters in Lewis Carroll's two books, *Alice's Adventures in Wonderland* and *Through the Looking-Glass*, are particularly relevant to a book on the changing views of successful management at the end of a disastrous, crazy, incredibly exciting but revolutionary century, in which the world, with its social, political and moral values, has been turned upside down. They were published in 1865 and 1872 respectively, and marked a turning-point in children's literature, which finally became fun as well as instructive. Charles Dodgson adopted the name of Lewis Carroll for his non-professional writing long before he invented 'Alice'. Under his own name he published learned books on mathematics, which, so the story goes, Queen

Victoria received with amazement in response to her order for all the rest of the author's works, after she had enjoyed *Alice's Adventures in Wonderland*. Instead of enchanting tales full of fantasy, she was presented with such titles as *Condensation of Determinants* and *The Fifth Book of Euclid treated Algebraically, so far as it relates to Commensurable Magnitudes*.

The world in which Charles Dodgson lived was still relatively stable, but both at home and abroad there were felt the first tremors of those cataclysmic changes which were eventually to blast the world apart. Sociological, political, industrial and technological revolution was in the air, though few realised perhaps how savagely those winds of change would blow, nor how soon.

We, too, live in a world of incredible, and exponential, change: *economically and politically*, we are seeing the emergence of the Far Eastern countries as a major world force. It is worth remembering the disturbing fact that there are over six hundred million Chinese entering their industrial age, and they are not all going to be making wooden sandals.

To give one example of *technological* change, the first practical industrial robot was introduced in the '60s. By 1982 there were approximately 32,000 robots being used in the USA alone. Today, there are more than 20,000,000. As Steven Wright, an American comedian, has put it, 'I have a microwave fireplace. You can lay down in front of the fire all night in eight minutes.'

And as regards *industrial or commercial* change, it is estimated that less than half the workforce in the industrial world will be holding full-time jobs in organisations by the beginning of the twenty-first century. Those full-timers or insiders will be the new minority.

What is more, with flatter structures, offering less opportunity for advancement, and looser ways of shaping an organisation, demanding greater need for flexibility and mobility, the demarcation between 'managers' and 'employees' is breaking down and becoming blurred. In a very real sense, all managers are employees, and all employees managers—of their careers, their time and their aspirations. So although *Past Tense, Future Per-*

fect, as the subtitle suggests, is aimed at managers, this group now contains a larger, more varied group of people, encompassing many more grades or levels, than has been the case until quite recently.

The parallels with the age in which Lewis Carroll, or Charles Dodgson, lived are there, and it is therefore fitting, perhaps, that his vivid and fantastic characters should serve as vehicles for lessons on how to succeed in this latest global revolution.

I have started each chapter with a passage from one of his two 'Alice' books, of a length which, I hope, will give a good portrait of the character concerned. There is some explanation of the relevance of the passages to the chapter's theme, but readers of 'Alice', and hopefully readers of this book, will have imagination enough to see the connexion, and often the relevance is glimpsed like the sun bursting through clouds, rather than stars scrutinised through a telescope.

I hope you find it useful—and enjoyable—for it is written for those who need help in making sense of today's world of work, and especially for those within that large group of men and women who understand and sympathise with words taken from both of Carroll's books: 'Alice was beginning to get very tired ... then she began looking about and noticed that what could be seen from the old room was quite common and uninteresting, but that all the rest was as different as possible.'

PART ONE

THE CHANGING WORLD OF WORK

CHAPTER 1

'I Look Up to Him'
The employees' view

'Where do you come from?' said the Red Queen. 'And where are you going? Look up, speak nicely, and don't twiddle your fingers all the time.'

Alice attended to all these directions, and explained, as well as she could, that she had lost her way.

'I don't know what you mean by *your* way,' said the Queen: 'all the ways about here belong to *me*—' . . . Just at this moment, somehow or other, they began to run.

Alice never could quite make out, in thinking it over afterwards, how it was that they began: all she remembers is that they were running hand in hand, and the Queen went so fast that it was all she could do to keep up with her: and still the Queen kept crying 'Faster!' but Alice felt she *could not* go faster, though she had no breath left to say so.

The most curious part of the thing was, that the trees and the other things round them never changed their places at all: however fast they went, they never seemed to pass anything . . . 'Are we nearly there?' Alice managed to pant out at last.

'Nearly there!' the Queen repeated. 'Why, we passed it ten minutes ago! Faster!' And they ran on . . . till suddenly, just as Alice was getting quite exhausted, they stopped, and she found herself sitting on the ground, breathless and giddy.

The Queen propped her up against a tree, and said kindly, 'You may rest a little now.'

Alice looked round her in great surprise. 'Why, I do believe we've been under this tree all the time! Everything's just as it was!'

'Of course it is,' said the Queen: 'what would you have it?'

'Well, in *our* country,' said Alice, still panting a little, 'you'd generally get to somewhere else—if you ran very fast for a long time, as we've been doing.'

'A slow sort of country!' said the Queen. 'Now, *here*, you see, it takes all the running *you* can do, to keep in the same place. If you want to get somewhere else, you must run at least twice as fast as that!'

*   *   *

To be employed is to be at risk; to be employable is to be secure. One indication of how widespread the Alice Principle is becoming is that in recent years the lot of employees at all levels has changed almost completely. These differences can be summed up in seven ways:

No one owes you a living

They never have, I suppose, but we have sometimes liked to think they do. I remember talking to a manager of a well-known high street retailing chain who said that for years he thought there was someone at Head Office whose job was to plan the careers and personal development of most managers, and of course his in particular. He eventually realised that this was a nonsense, and that the only person responsible for his career was himself.

That is a salutary lesson, and a new one for many people. If I want my career to develop, I must take responsibility for this, plan what I want to do and then seek to equip myself for attaining my goal, preferably with the help of my current employer. The job I do is for my employer, to whom I owe such things as loyalty, time and those management skills expected of me, but I owe it to myself to set my goals and attain them in the most effective way possible.

Careers change

With every technological change, the need for some jobs reduces, and sometimes disappears. How many people today remember comptometer operators? Yet thousands of people up and down the country, especially women, were employed in this job not so many years ago and were replaced, quite rapidly, with the advent and spread of the computer.

We need to try to gauge the current trends, to assess which are going to be seminal and permanent, and plan and prepare accordingly. There are many gurus to help us, of whom Charles Handy in Britain is perhaps the most accessible as well as being one of the most prescient. Having read *The Age of Unreason* I enjoyed, more recently, *The Empty Raincoat*, and realised how many of the pictures he paints are now coming off the canvas and taking life. A central theme of his book is his concept of the sigmoid curve—like the letter 'S' on its side. Those organisations—and individuals—survive and flourish, he argues, who are preparing to face future changes and challenges *at precisely the time when they appear to be doing well* on their current, most static, course.

The implication for us is that to grow our future career, we need to be learning new skills even when we seem set on success if we continue as we are. If we are *not* set on success, when redundancy or sudden unemployment trigger questions as to whether or not we are in the 'right career', we very quickly learn to query the currency of our skills.

The evidence is there, then, that the remainder of the 1990s will see a growing trend in mid-life career changes as people increasingly seek to meet changing demands for work.

People change

In a 1992 survey by the Roper Organisation, 45 per cent of US workers said they would change their careers if they could. Numerous recent studies suggest the UK is no different.

In my experience people change their career in varying degrees—they may stay in the same industry but change their function; they may change the scope of their role; they may move into a different industry; they may move from the public to the private sector or from employment to self-employment—and they may make these changes at any time of life. Commitments, priorities, personal goals and the balance between home and family all change over time, and they govern the part a career plays in our lives.

Change is permanent, and quicker each year

Like most people I wish it were not so and that, once in a while, the world would stop and I could get off. However, economic competitive pressure from the Third World, the exponential growth of science and technology, the relentless desire for better living standards, and the realisation that the environment is not a victim to be raped but a partner to be respected and courted, all contribute to the scope and pace of change that surrounds us.

And change costs.

You can see it in the faces of the people next to you on the bus or the Underground—the way people, who are presumably efficient workers and normal partners and parents, become zombies as they commute between work space and leisure space each morning and evening.

Of course, there is no anodyne to taking risks: with the old order clearly passing and with those jobs traditionally held to be 'safe'—in the civil service and local government, in the armed forces, the utility companies and even in the Church—all now subject to regular re-engineering and redundancy programmes, it is clearly time for some new thinking about jobs.

But how? It is said that half the jobs men and women will work at in America in the year 2000 don't yet exist, so how can I know which direction to take?

Attitude to change is vital

One way is to prepare the right 'mind set' for change.

One of the reasons why it remains true that 'if you want to get something done, give it to a busy person' is that the busy person has two key attributes: an acute awareness of time management and an ability to take on new things, to see opportunities in new situations and constantly to juggle priorities accordingly. It is this attitude to change, and in particular to the process of transition leading up to change, which determines whether we can manage changes when they are coming at us from all sides at once. This is very much the case when we believe the changes are likely to impact on the job or career that we hold dear.

Giles was Britain's best-loved cartoonist, says Peter Tory in his authorised biography, *Giles—A Life in Cartoons*. He refers to the move Giles made, at the age of 27, from *Reynolds News*, a left-wing Sunday journal, to the *Daily Express*, a nationally influential newspaper. Giles resisted the change, saying, 'I am very happy where I am. I would be very unhappy if I changed.' It would probably be true to say, said an observer, that 'having made the change he became for a time a very unhappy man. He missed the old familiar faces and the old comfortable setting. He was uncertain, diffident and thoroughly miserable. Then all of a sudden he changed. The old certainty of touch returned.' What caused this change? Simply that readers had begun to write to him in their masses, telling him how much they liked him. On this observation, external influences played a very important part in shaping Giles' attitude to the change from journal to newspaper.

In another book, this time an autobiography called *Conflict of Loyalty*, Lord Howe refers to his early days with the Bow Group when he was at Cambridge University, and later as a barrister in the 1950s. The title of a publication of the one-nation group was 'Change is our ally'. He held an internal conviction that change was a good thing and presented opportunities, *if* there was a readiness to accept it like a friend.

Successful change involves creativity and innovation

One could sum up what will be required of those who will be successful in their careers in the next century in the phrase *'right brain or left behind'*. The right brain is the creative, innovative side of us, and uses our imagination to help us towards new ways of approaching what we have to do. It is the opposite of the approach outlined in the passage about the Red Queen in *Through the Looking-Glass*, quoted above. With the Red Queen, 'it takes all the running you can do to stay in the same place'. Not surprisingly, exhaustion follows. Does this seem familiar in the way you yourself are expected to work? If so, there is a danger of being 'left behind' in the search for career success.

Creative organisations and individuals are now preparing for a better way to achieve successful careers by being more innovative in the way jobs and the way time spent at work are structured. Now, as well as what are sometimes called 'proper jobs', we have portfolio jobs, homeworking and telecottages.

We have a huge growth in consultancies, with functions traditionally performed in-house being outsourced or externalised—dreadful words for a simple practice—and, consequently, a blurring of the edges between client and supplier.

As well as a 35-hour week plus, we have flexitime, job-sharing, term-time jobs, weekend jobs, four ten-hour days a week or eight-day fortnights, annual-hours contracts, zero-hour contracts, time banking (accumulating holiday entitlements over several years) and individual-hour contracts agreed between individuals and their bosses each week or each month.

A few real-life examples may help to illustrate this new creativity and flexibility:

A 52-year-old executive in the oil industry decided that redundancy provided a unique opportunity to do something completely different in a role which would provide more job satisfaction. He approached 150 organisations in the voluntary sector and his perseverance and a willingness to work, initially on a voluntary basis, resulted in a paid position as the development director of the Hawk and Owl Trust—a job providing interest, job satisfaction and an opportunity to involve the family.

An engineer faced with the choice of being a technical specialist or moving up the management ladder, decided he was attracted to neither and took time out to identify his skills. He decided that analysing complex problems, evaluating options, presenting solutions and persuading people were skills common to both engineers and lawyers. He had been involved with the legal side of engineering as a result of his work on construction projects and patents and decided to take the plunge and study for three years, first for a diploma in law and then on the Bar Vocational Course. He specialised in construction law, ranging from contracts for home extensions to disputes involving bridges, oil rigs and shops, thus building on his knowledge gained as a chartered engineer.

A 30-year-old maths graduate, who made the all-too-easy move into a well-paid job with a multinational blue-chip company, realised that she was on a 'career conveyor belt'. She had little pride in her work and no enthusiasm for the aims of the organisation. Voluntary redundancy offered her the time and space to think. The opportunity of an extended trip travelling around Asia gave her an improved perspective on what mattered in her life. Her search for a new career was a full-time four-month project involving an analysis of her values and transferable skills and eventually she chose to focus on an area connected to her lifelong passion for music. She says that what prepared her best for the career change into arts administration was meeting and talking with people employed in similar positions: these meetings filled her with enthusiasm and provided her with the knowledge of the sector necessary for credibility at interviews.

Since the average person today can expect to have between three and six career changes in his or her lifetime, I find these examples encouraging, since they demonstrate that, increasingly, if people are prepared to take time to find out what they really want and make the effort to pursue it, the career opportunity will emerge which best matches their skills, their values and in which they can make a real contribution. As Goethe said, 'Whatever you can do or dream you can, begin it. Boldness has truth, beauty and magic in it.'

Successful careers in the future will involve willingness to take risks

The sort of risks, that is, taken by those managers who sacrifice much to take a diploma in management studies or a master of business administration degree, or by those young people who take a year before university to work overseas.

A young child in the Roman world would learn the value of two key attitudes from his or her paterfamilias or father—first *pietas*, which was a devotion to the gods, the state and also to the family, which are essentially external attributes; and second, *gravitas*, which involved having a sense of gravity, dignity and responsibility, which are essentially internal attributes. In this ancient world *both* these attitudes were equally important and would be appealed to when any new situation arose.

An organisation in the automotive industry, about to undergo organisational changes, conducted a survey amongst its UK staff across several sites. They discovered that, as with their forebears in ancient Rome, the staff incorporated both external and internal attitudes to change, in varying degrees. The response was that 20 per cent said they expected the changes to be made and wanted the company to get on and implement them. Seventy per cent said that they acknowledged the need for the change but needed help and reassurance along the way as the transition progressed. Ten per cent said that they did not like what they heard and were unwilling to change. In other words, there was a minority in the vanguard of change who could imagine themselves in the future; the vast majority who could see the future and were prepared to go along with the management for the present, and finally a hard core group who were living in the past, and were not prepared to take risks to protect and enhance their future. The company knew it could not impose changes on this last group and, in the end, there was a mutual agreement with them to leave.

Risk is never easy, but in the future it will be increasingly inevitable.

To sum up, then: those who, to whatever extent, try to shape their careers within the above seven parameters will, I believe, not just be employed: they will be employable, with transferable skills, new skills, and an innovative and creative approach to the fascinating and ever-changing kaleidoscope of jobs and careers in the future. In short, using their creativity, their right brain, to plan their career, they will be right for the demands of the next century, and certainly not left behind.

CHAPTER 2

An Appetite for Change
The employers' view

The Walrus and the Carpenter
  Were walking close at hand;
They wept like anything to see
  Such quantities of sand:
'If this were only cleared away,'
  They said, 'it *would* be grand!'

         *   *   *

'O Oysters, come and walk with us!'
  The Walrus did beseech.
'A pleasant walk, a pleasant talk,
  Along the briny beach:
We cannot do with more than four,
  To give a hand to each.'

The eldest Oyster looked at him.
  But never a word he said:
The eldest Oyster winked his eye,
  And shook his heavy head—
Meaning to say he did not choose
  To leave the oyster-bed.

But four young oysters hurried up,
  All eager for the treat:
Their coats were brushed, their faces washed,
  Their shoes were clean and neat—
And this was odd, because, you know,
  They hadn't any feet.

Four other Oysters followed them,
  And yet another four;
And thick and fast they came at last,
  And more, and more, and more—
All hopping through the frothy waves,
  And scrambling to the shore.

The Walrus and the Carpenter
  Walked on a mile or so,
And then they rested on a rock
  Conveniently low:
And all the little Oysters stood
  And waited in a row.

'The time has come,' the Walrus said,
  'To talk of many things:
Of shoes—and ships—and sealing-wax—
  Of cabbages—and kings—
And why the sea is boiling hot—
  And whether pigs have wings.'

'But wait a bit,' the Oysters cried,
  'Before we have our chat;
For some of us are out of breath,
  And all of us are fat!'
'No hurry!' said the Carpenter.
  They thanked him much for that.

'A loaf of bread,' the Walrus said,
  'Is what we chiefly need:
Pepper and vinegar besides
  Are very good indeed—
Now if you're ready, Oysters dear,
  We can begin to feed.'

'But not on us!' the Oysters cried,
  Turning a little blue,
'After such kindness, that would be

A dismal thing to do!'
'The night is fine,' the Walrus said
'Do you admire the view?

'It was so kind of you to come!
   And you are very nice!'
The Carpenter said nothing but
   'Cut us another slice:
I wish you were not quite so deaf—
   I've had to ask you twice!'

'It seems a shame,' the Walrus said,
   'To play them such a trick,
After we've brought them out so far,
   And made them trot so quick!'
The Carpenter said nothing but
   'The butter's spread too thick!'

'I weep for you,' the Walrus said,
   'I deeply sympathise.'
With sobs and tears he sorted out
   Those of the largest size
Holding his pocket-handkerchief
   Before his streaming eyes.

'O Oysters,' said the Carpenter.
   'You've had a pleasant run!
Shall we be trotting home again?'
   But answer came there none—
And this was scarcely odd, because
   They'd eaten every one.

*　　*　　*

One of Vice-President Dan Quayle's less painful slips of the tongue was 'It's a question of whether we're going to go forward into the future, or past into the back.'

I imagine almost every chief executive or board of management these days wants to avoid going 'past into the back', but understanding the values, the motivation of the people who will have to implement change—the sort of people whose approach to change we saw in the last chapter—and matching these to corporate values and goals, is crucial if their plans for the future are to succeed. Clearly these corporate objectives and values will vary in different types of organisation, and will attract different kinds of employees. To take three examples:

Unilever, an Anglo-Dutch conglomerate, has a long history of taking a consistent approach to the management of change. On the dimension of its turnover of £28 billion, if Unilever were classified as a country, it would rank around fortieth out of the 180 countries in the United Nations. Reference is often made to the Unilever 'glue', which gives the organisation a global set of values. A key component is excellence and concern for staff, and this is where individual values blend with corporate values. The emphasis is very much on the word 'global', for typically, at a management development workshop, some 18 nationalities might be represented in the 30 people present. Two specific values within Unilever are consistency and openness.

On the other hand, City financial institutions undergoing rapid growth may have little formal management structure and, while operating throughout Europe, may manage the hundreds of people in the UK as though they were part of a start-up business. The kind of person who would be happy in this type of environment is likely to be very unlike the Unilever employee, with different, though no less clear, corporate values. Emphasis tends to be on individuals being focused, with responsibilities in a constantly changing market-place taking priority over job descriptions. Discussions by managers and personnel staff about individuals' careers and development are central to the process.

The chief executive of a Mental Health NHS Trust asked each management team member of the Trust to present what it was that drove them in their work. Everyone at the top reinforced the message that management was there to help people in the organisation do their work better, so corporate values were set by consensus, with staff feeling that they were themselves valued, and seeing this as the organisational norm. The Trust introduced an approach to quality based on the theories of W. Edwards Deming, the revolutionary American guru who, earlier this

century, advocated the treatment of workers as partners rather than adversaries, and believed in quality rather than quantity production. (Ironically, after the Second World War his ideas were taken up by the Japanese rather than in his own country, leading to the total quality management concept in Japan and that country's phenomenal economic recovery.)

The employers' view, therefore, is to some extent a reflection of the employees' view, balancing it, but also modifying it, as the organisation itself is modified by pressures for change. As the investments advertisement said: 'You think you understand the situation, but what you don't understand is that the situation just changed.'

For example, flatter structures are the result of organisational, operational and financial need, but they put pressure on individuals in relation to their own development: some see the job opportunities disappearing and carp; others view *carpe diem* as a better watchword, and seize the opportunity to get true empowerment and grow in responsibility and achievement.

In this situation the wise employer will respond by taking the initiative and seeking to adapt his or her approach accordingly, the aim being to manage in new ways so that individual staff are WISE:

- WELL-PREPARED because they are coached and taught to take ownership;
- INSPIRED to meet new goals because of the leadership given to them;
- SUPPORTED when things go wrong and mistakes are made;
- ENCOURAGED to continue those things that are going well.

Some managers are unwilling or unable to adapt their approach in this way, and they—and the companies they run—are going to have problems in the future. Others *are* willing and find that their job descriptions are nothing like they used to be. The description may now be written in terms of the *aims* of the job, not its particular content, with an increasing emphasis on what their *team* is doing and what the *outputs* should be.

Employers are shifting from the idea of a 'job to be performed' to 'work to be done'. Come the revolution—and it is coming— people will no longer have so many company yardsticks by which to rate themselves (like rank or grade or even job title); the focus will be much more individual (their view of their own skill development, marketability and self-worth).

Senior executives will need to know their people's capabilities as well as their own, what they want and where they need to develop, and ensure opportunities are available for them to achieve. In return managers will be more individually *account- able* in their area: it will be *their* customers and *their* decisions.

This is not stress, this is exciting . . .

. . . but not for everybody.

As a recruitment consultant friend of mine put it: 'How can an existing management team suddenly slip through 180 degrees and do things differently from that which they used to do?' The problem is that organisations have great difficulty sometimes in making changes, whether by growing suitable executives intern- ally, or by 'organically' implementing what is necessary. External expertise, through appointing new managers, or through using consultants to develop internal vision, is needed—though this in itself may create problems because companies going through change need to preserve their central ethos (e.g. customer friendliness in banks) while needing to change their culture (e.g. more holes in the wall = fewer cashiers and = less face-to-face contact with customers).

An interesting current development among employers is that many now expect managers to be more adventurous than conservative, possessing rather more 'soft' skills such as inherent intellectual ability, flexibility and personality, with relevant but not necessarily directly-related experience. The days of the ruthless executive, to the right of Genghis Khan and usually financially orientated, are distinctly numbered, like those many whom they themselves exiled into redundancy . . .

Information-sharing is another key factor in the new perspective from the top: if effective action necessitates cutting out several layers of management to decrease the cost base and focus the enterprise, many more people need to have good information. Traditionally this has been a source of management power, but senior executives can no longer manage by exclusive ownership of information, since there are far more people reporting to them than ever in the past.

Listening—another soft skill—is also important: there is no longer a right to be right on everything, but rather a need to recognise that expertise can reside outside an individual executive.

One striking new feature coming through into the market is that it is less ageist than it was in the bull market several years ago, with a greater need for wisdom, maturity and judgement, at least in companies with a culture and style which value these qualities.

The employers' view is therefore very varied, balancing that of the employee but differing from it, with many different models to evaluate. But they all have 'an appetite for change', a phrase with sinister overtones for the picture presented in the poem about the Walrus and the Carpenter quoted above, where the assets—the oysters—are literally stripped of their life by being consumed. Asset-stripping is not much in vogue these days, but it is not unknown, with deafness to entreaty or reason, trickery, and bogus remorse accompanied by fatuous platitudes, all in evidence. I confess to having taken part myself in an exercise which was not too far distant from the machiavellian and destructive scheming of the Walrus and the Carpenter, when, as personnel director, I liaised with one of the best-known management consultancies in the world in a process they had devised to assist in downsizing. The 'natives' (I've always wondered why oysters are called this) were as friendly and unsuspecting as they are in 'Alice', and co-operated in listing their job tasks, the amount of time the jobs took, their relative importance, and the risk to the business if they were not done. After that, of course, it was a simple task to add up the man, or woman, years of unnecessary or questionable jobs, and reduce the appropriate number of staff through redundancy. It was a sad business—asset-stripping or downsizing always is—and I'm sure a few lightly-felt tears were briefly shed, but it did not stop the process.

A significant outcome, however, was that the exercise destroyed the trust and confidence of the employees in the company totally and permanently—when the company had been known locally as one of the best employers around. The bitterness was perhaps all the more because the employees realised that they had been the cause of their own destruction—exactly like the oysters, in fact. After this event there were no volunteers and too many who, like the eldest Oyster, 'did not choose to leave the oyster-bed'. Surely in these days of supposed enlightenment there must be a better way of shaping an organisation into the right size, enabling the victims to keep their dignity and identity rather than allowing them to be (literally) eaten alive?

If no such way can be found by employers—and, while there are encouraging trends in the short term, I believe the jury is out as to longer-term ones—then William Spooner's own slip of the tongue may be a better one than Dan Quayle's: 'You will find as you grow older that the weight of rages will press harder and harder upon the employer.'

PART TWO

LEADERSHIP

CHAPTER 3

Follow my Leader?
The nature of leadership

At this moment, Five, who had been anxiously looking across the garden, called out 'The Queen! The Queen!' and the three gardeners instantly threw themselves flat upon their faces. There was a sound of many footsteps, and Alice looked round, eager to see the Queen.

First came ten soldiers carrying clubs; these were all shaped like the three gardeners, oblong and flat, with their hands and feet at the corners; next the ten courtiers; these were ornamented all over with diamonds, and walked two by two, as the soldiers did. After these came the royal children; there were ten of them, and the little dears came jumping merrily along hand in hand, in couples: they were all ornamented with hearts. Next came the guests, mostly Kings and Queens . . . Then followed the Knave of Hearts, carrying the King's crown on a crimson velvet cushion; and, last of all this grand procession, came THE KING AND QUEEN OF HEARTS.

Alice was rather doubtful whether she ought not to lie down on her face like the three gardeners, but she could not remember ever having heard of such a rule at processions; 'and besides, what would be the use of a procession,' thought she, 'if people had all to lie down on their faces, so that they couldn't see it?' So she stood still where she was, and waited.

When the procession came opposite to Alice, they all stopped and looked at her, and the Queen said severely, 'Who is this?' She said it to the Knave of Hearts, who only bowed and smiled in reply.

'Idiot!' said the Queen, tossing her head impatiently; and, turning to Alice, she went on, 'What's your name, child?'

'My name is Alice, so please your Majesty,' said Alice very politely; but she added, to herself, 'Why, they're only a pack of cards, after all. I needn't be afraid of them!'

'And who are *these*?' said the Queen, pointing to the three gardeners . . .

'How should *I* know?' said Alice, surprised at her own courage. 'It's no business of *mine*.'

The Queen turned crimson with fury, and, after glaring at her for a moment like a wild beast, screamed 'Off with her head! Off—'

'Nonsense!' said Alice, very loudly and decidedly, and the Queen was silent.

The King laid his hand upon her arm, and timidly said 'Consider, my dear: she is only a child!' . . . turning to the rose-tree, [the Queen] went on, 'What *have* you been doing here?'

'May it please your Majesty,' said Two, in a very humble tone . . . 'we were trying—'

'*I* see!' said the Queen, who had meanwhile been examining the roses. 'Off with their heads!' and the procession moved on, three of the soldiers remaining behind to execute the unfortunate gardeners, who ran to Alice for protection.

'You sha'n't be beheaded!' said Alice, and she put them into a large flower-pot that stood near. The three soldiers wandered about for a minute or two, looking for them, and then quietly marched off after the others.

'Are their heads off?' shouted the Queen.

'Their heads are gone, if it please your Majesty!' the soldiers shouted in reply . . .

'How do you like the Queen?' said the [Cheshire] Cat in a low voice.

'Not at all,' said Alice: 'she's so extremely—' Just then she noticed that the Queen was close behind her listening: so she went on, '—likely to win, that it's hardly worth finishing the game.'

The Queen smiled and passed on.

*   *   *

The Queen of Hearts is not a model of good leadership: she is a bully, full of bombast but quick to back off when challenged, and snide in her way of creeping up on people and eavesdropping. Her only virtue is that nobody takes any notice of her tendency towards decapitation. Better models for today's environment would be Alexandre Auguste Ledru-Rollin who, in Paris in the nineteenth century, was found at the back of a mob supporting the policies he was advocating. When asked why he was there and not at the front, he replied, 'Ah well! I am their leader, I really had to follow them!' Or Dag Hammarskjoeld, who said when he was General Secretary of the United Nations, 'Your position never gives you the right to command. It imposes on you the duty of living your life so that others can receive orders without being humiliated.'

My favourite description of leadership, however, comes from Lao-Tse, living in China in about 500 BC:

A leader is best
When people scarcely know that he exists,
Not so good when they blindly obey and acclaim him.
Worse when they despise him.
'Fail to honour people
They fail to honour you.'
But to a good leader, who talks little,
When his work is done, his aim fulfilled,
They will all say, 'We did this ourselves.'[1]

We have all seen the striking picture posters on office walls with a *bon mot* regarding some aspect of business: 'Leaders are like eagles, they don't flock, you find them one at a time'. A pack of horses pounds away in a cloud of dust to the caption: 'The speed of the leader determines the rate of the pack'. However, one statement about leadership, which caught my attention the other day, was inscribed on a piece of rock to be placed on a desk: 'Real leaders are ordinary people with extraordinary determination'. The rock was made to look like a tombstone, but the sentiment that everyone can be a leader is alive and well, and should stay so, for it is very relevant to today's business culture.

In 1995 a survey was carried out by MORI. It consisted of

706 telephone interviews conducted between 3 and 17 January
with main board directors, using a structured questionnaire.
The sample was drawn randomly from listings of the top 500
companies by turnover, in each of six UK regions. The aim
was to explore what business leaders felt about the nature and
requirements of business leadership and to identify the essential
characteristics and attitudes that would shape the leaders of the
future.

More than 80 per cent saw a leader primarily as a *motivator*,
who had the ability to get others involved and stimulate their
interest. Over 30 per cent saw the leader as an *innovator* concerned with the creation of new ideas or a new vision. The word
'coach' was selected by 32 per cent of respondents, as being
generally associated with a non-autocratic style. The most auto-
cratic term, 'boss', usually associated with control or possibly
domination, was selected by only 14 per cent of the sample.

Going deeper into the characteristics of business leaders, the
ability to motivate people reporting to them was again top of the
list, rated by 98 per cent of respondents. The next two most
strongly rated characteristics were the ability 'to attract the best
people to their team' (87 per cent), and 'to turn visions into
reality' (88 per cent). In these qualities there emerges the picture
of a leader in terms of a person with strength of vision, and with
the charisma or power to motivate others to share that vision
and ensure that it can then be implemented. Curiously enough,
respondents did not consider that good company performance
was necessarily an indicator of a successful business leader!

The 1994–95 Ashridge Management Index was produced by
the research group at Ashridge Management College. A total of
401 managers who had attended Ashridge programmes responded
to a questionnaire: 20 per cent of them were at Board level
in their organisations and a further 45 per cent were in senior
management. The Index is repeated annually, and is not so much
about what it is like working for a particular organisation, as about
what it is like to be a manager in today's business environment.

Over 25 per cent of managers were concerned about the issues of organisational change and the difficulties of introducing new ways of working. Twenty-three per cent saw the changing nature of the managerial role as their biggest challenge, and 90 per cent expressed concern about developing their future roles as functional specialists, agreeing with the statement 'I am expected to be both a generalist and a specialist'.

When it came to the vision of the leaders, these managers reported a lack of shared vision concerning the development and implementation of strategy. Strategic plans tended to be developed by the few for the many. Only 33 per cent believed that most people in their organisation understood its strategic goals, and fewer than 25 per cent worked in organisations where the strategic plan was distributed to all the staff.

I am reminded of one of Scott Adams' 'Dilbert' cartoons, where the dialogue goes like this:

'Here's the company vision and business plan.'
' "Vision-empowered employees working towards a common plan" —sounds good . . . But the business plan is blank.'
'It's confidential.'
'How am I supposed to know what to do?'
'I'll yell at you if you do the wrong thing.'
'I thought I was empowered.'
'Don't be so literal.'
'I'll just keep doing what I was doing.'
'No!!! You fool!!!' . . .
'We're doomed, aren't we?'
'I don't know—I haven't seen the business plan.'[2]

There is so often in organisations a credibility gap between what senior management want, or at least say they want, and the acceptance and 'ownership' of this by the workforce. I saw these words on a card in a bookshop recently: 'I'm sure you believe you understand what I've said. But I'm not convinced that what you heard is what I meant.' It is the task of the leader to help bridge that credibility, or communications, gap.

When I taught at Sundridge Park we used to define leadership as *that part of a manager's activities by which he influences the behaviour of individuals and groups towards a desired result, and which depends upon the human relations skills and personality of the manager to meet the intrinsic and extrinsic needs of the group he leads.*

Sadly, it doesn't often happen. A survey carried out in 1994 by Sundridge Park Management Centre looked at the differences between how managers rated the importance of various attributes of a successful business leader, and how far they perceived their present CEO as having them. There was little correlation, with the biggest gaps in:

Ability to build effective teams	should have: 96 per cent (the highest attribute) CEO has: 50 per cent
Knows how to listen	should have: 93 per cent CEO has: 44 per cent
Motivated by power	should have: 35 per cent CEO has: 59 per cent
Motivated by money	should have: 17 per cent CEO has: 40 per cent
Capable of making decisions on his own	should have: 87 per cent CEO has: 66 per cent

So what *are* the qualities of a good business leader today? A 'summary of summaries' would seem to indicate that top of the list are:

● PERSISTENCE
● SELF-KNOWLEDGE
● WILLINGNESS TO TAKE RISKS
● WILLINGNESS TO ACCEPT LOSSES
● COMMITMENT
● CONSISTENCY
● CHALLENGE
● PERPETUAL LEARNING THROUGH EXPERIENCE AND A WIDE RANGE OF RESOURCES OR MEDIA

It is interesting that 'charisma' is rarely mentioned, but the list has recently become extended by softer or more 'touchy feely' qualities:

● ACKNOWLEDGING AND SHARING UNCERTAINTY
● EMBRACING ERROR
● RESPONDING TO THE FUTURE
● BECOMING INTERPERSONALLY COMPETENT (LISTENING, NURTURING, COPING WITH CONFLICTS)

And it is the use of more colourful and imaginative language to describe what leaders do, or what kind of people they are, that is a definite trend: thus Sir John Harvey-Jones, in *Making Things Happen*, describes leadership as 'art, not science', and Warren Bennis talks of leaders 'embracing error' and 'managing the dream'; Bennis also says, almost poetically, that becoming a leader is like beauty or art, not easy, but like becoming a doctor or poet, with essential ingredients consisting of Guiding Vision, Passion, Integrity, Trust, Curiosity and Daring.[3]

The leaders of tomorrow, this suggests, will have far more people knowledge, both about others and—themselves.

It has been said that if your goal horizons are one year, you plant corn; if ten years, you plant trees; if one hundred years, you plant people. As companies begin to invest in people as

standard practice, the role of employers will be dramatically
changed because it will demand a recognition of everyone's
involvement and contribution.

Sir Ranulph Fiennes, in his book *Mind over Matter*, outlines
his approach to leadership. He says his policy is always to choose
self-reliant, strong characters for his team since they are more
likely to push themselves against great odds. The downside of
this is that such people are invariably independent-minded, often
antagonistic and nearly always critically outspoken. He goes on
to say, 'I need to have my own way, but secretly so. I must
appear to be democratic, to listen to advice, patiently to discuss
criticisms to my suggested course of action and, whenever a
better course is suggested, to go with it at once and to give open
credit for it.' There are remarkable echoes here of the Lao-Tse
description of leadership above . . .

People at any level in an organisation can have ideas which
may take them beyond the boundaries of their current job. Each
individual can both motivate and be motivated by colleagues.
But if this potential is to be realised they all need leaders who
can act as catalysts for change.

Not, of course, that business leaders of tomorrow will ignore
the achievement of hard economic success: Michael Porter's *The
Competitive Advantage of Nations* looks at national economic
performance, and what makes some nations advance and become
highly competitive in global markets. He writes, 'the success of
leaders depends on possessing insights into opportunities and the
tools to exploit them . . . Leaders do not accept constraints and
know that they can change the nature of outcomes. They are in
a position to perceive something about reality that has escaped
others, and have the courage to act.'

But it is on people management that the successful leaders will
focus: in the sporting world, Mike Brearley, former England
cricket captain, sets out his views on leadership in his book, *The
Art of Captaincy*. A leader's contribution in cricket is crucial
because there are three overriding considerations: the time-span
of the game and the changing tempo within it; the variations in

conditions which are beyond his control (weather, nature of pitch, character of umpires, crowd temperament and so on); and the variety of roles within a single team. 'A captain must get the best out of his team by helping them to play together without suppressing flair and uniqueness,' he says.

Implicit in these words is an understanding and vision about what the team can achieve if allowed to perform at its best. Vision, and the ability to communicate it to the individuals in the team, are equally important.

The key qualities here are intuition and courage to act on that intuition while creating the right atmosphere and environment. If the leader finds the right challenges, Brearley suggests, he or she must then generate the conditions where 'innovation grows out of pressure and challenge'.

In *The Leadership Equation*, L. and N. Barr go through various case studies in leadership and management, using the Myers-Briggs Type Indicator (MBTI is a psychometric instrument which asks a series of questions to help identify people's preferences in four areas: how they relate to other people; how they absorb data; how they make decisions; and how they organise their time— see Chapter 22 below). In their view, leadership requires 'people savvy' and a personal awareness of 'the privilege of service'. They base their research and case studies around the premise that power increases in a leader as that leader empowers others.

This is taking Brearley's art of captaincy and aligning it to the world of business, while introducing another dimension— self-knowledge. 'Leadership,' say Barr and Barr, 'over the long term, requires self-knowledge. You can learn managerial functions and develop managerial skills, but sustained leadership requires self-knowledge, self-realisation, self-discipline and self-development ... Those who would be in a position of leading people must first develop themselves.'

We have come a long way from the Queen of Hearts' approach to personal leadership. Leaders at the top of organisations today realise that in developing an atmosphere and environment in which Fiennes' 'self-reliant, strong characters' can flourish, they

will be releasing leadership abilities at all levels in 'ordinary
people with extraordinary determination', as the inscription said
on that piece of rock.

In August 1975 Gore Vidal wrote in *The Listener*: '[Commer-
cialism] is doing well that which should not be done at all.'[4] In
the '90s business leaders cannot survive under that philosophy—
they would certainly lose their heads, or at least their jobs. Leadership today is not so much a regal and privileged procession by
the Queen of Hearts as an exhilarating dance, joined in by all
and not just Rosabeth Moss Kanter's 'giants', and leaders need
to put their own meaning into Sydney Carter's words:

> 'Dance then whoever you may be,
> I am the lord of the dance,' said he,
> 'And I'll lead you all, wherever you may be,
> And I'll lead you all in the dance,' said he.[5]

CHAPTER 4

Twin Piques

Leadership and management

... turning a sharp corner, [Alice] came upon two fat little men ... the words of the old song kept ringing through her head like the ticking of a clock, and she could hardly help saying them out loud:

> 'Tweedledum and Tweedledee
>   Agreed to have a battle;
> For Tweedledum said Tweedledee
>   Had spoiled his nice new rattle.
>
> 'Just then flew down a monstrous crow,
>   As black as a tar-barrel;
> Which frightened both the heroes so,
>   They quite forgot their quarrel.'

'... I'd better be getting out of the wood,' [Alice said], 'for really it's coming on very dark. Do you think it's going to rain?'

Tweedledum spread a large umbrella over himself and his brother, and looked up into it. 'No, I don't think it is,' he said: 'at least—not under *here*. Nohow.'

'But it may rain *outside*?'

'It may—if it chooses,' said Tweedledee: 'we've no objection. Contrariwise.'

'Selfish things!' thought Alice, and she was just going to say

'Goodnight!' and leave them, when Tweedledum sprang out from under the umbrella, and seized her by the wrist.

'Do you see *that*?' he said, in a voice choking with passion, and his eyes grew large and yellow all in a moment, as he pointed with a trembling finger at a small white thing lying under the tree.

'It's only a rattle,' Alice said . . . 'only an old rattle—quite old and broken.'

'I knew it was!' cried Tweedledum, beginning to stamp about wildly and tear his hair. 'It's spoilt, of course!' Here he looked at Tweedledee, who immediately sat down on the ground, and tried to hide himself under the umbrella.

Alice laid her hand upon his arm, and said in a soothing tone, 'You needn't be so angry about an old rattle.'

'But it isn't old!' Tweedledum cried, in a greater fury than ever. 'It's new, I tell you—I bought it yesterday—my nice NEW RATTLE!' and his voice rose to a perfect scream . . .

'Of course you agree to have a battle?' Tweedledum said in a calmer tone.

'I suppose so,' the other sulkily replied, as he crawled out of the umbrella: 'only *she* must help us to dress up, you know.'

So the two brothers went off hand-in-hand into the wood, and returned in a minute with their arms full of things—such as bolsters, blankets, hearth-rugs, table-cloths, dish-covers and coal-scuttles . . .

'Do I look very pale?' said Tweedledum, coming up to have his helmet tied on. (He *called* it a helmet, though it certainly looked much more like a saucepan.)

'Well—yes—a *little*,' Alice replied gently.

'I'm very brave generally,' he went on in a low voice: 'only today I happen to have a headache.'

'And *I've* got a toothache!' said Tweedledee, who had overheard the remark. 'I'm far worse than you!'

'Then you'd better not fight today,' said Alice, thinking it a good opportunity to make peace.

'We *must* have a bit of a fight, but I don't care about going on long,' said Tweedledum. 'What's the time now?'

'Tweedledee looked at his watch, and said 'Half-past four.'

'Let's fight till six, and then have dinner,' said Tweedledum.

*   *   *

Field Marshal Lord Slim wrote in his memoirs, 'There is a difference between leadership and management.

'Leadership is of the spirit, compounded of personality and vision; its practice is an art. Management is of the mind, more a matter of accurate calculation, of methods, timetables and routines; its practice is a science. Managers are necessary, leaders are essential.'

The last chapter looked at modern views of leadership—and it is surprising, in that sense, how 'modern' Lord Slim's definition of leadership is. But many people don't think of themselves as leaders, and find it hard to take to themselves the inscription on that rock shaped like a tombstone: 'Real leaders are ordinary people with extraordinary determination'.

Managers, yes, but leaders?

So *is* there a difference between the two, and if so, what is it? Lord Slim seemed to think there was, and put it very elegantly. Others disagree, pointing out that it is all a matter of degree: certainly the definition of *leadership* in the last chapter implied that it was one part of a *manager*'s responsibilities: 'Leadership is that part of a manager's activities by which he influences the behaviour of individuals and groups towards a desired result. It depends upon the human relations skills and personality of the manager to meet the intrinsic and extrinsic needs of the group he leads.'

Others refer to the fact that leaders don't necessarily have to be the gung-ho, over-the-top, highly extrovert type represented in heroes and heroines from Biggles to Lady Thatcher. In the Bayeux tapestry, for example, there is a panel entitled 'King Harold leading his troops'—and he is at the back of the field, in a position he must have regarded as fairly secure . . . So it is possible to lead, not only from the front, but also from the middle ('come and join me in this project . . .') and from the back ('over to you . . . I'll keep a watching brief overall, and just keep me informed . . .'). With these latter two approaches, whether they amount to leadership or management is a nice point.

Some writers do, however, see a difference. Warren Bennis' views, for example, can be summarised thus:

MANAGER	LEADER
Administers	Innovates
Is a copy	Is an original
Maintains	Develops
Relies on control	Inspires trust
Short range	Long perspective
How? When?	What? Why?
Eye on bottom line	Eye on horizon
Initiates	Originates
Good soldier	Own person
Does things right	Does right things[1]

John Kotter puts more flesh on these pygmy bones; a précis of his views on *leadership* would list:

CREATING A CLEAR SENSE OF DIRECTION
- challenging people to question the status quo;
- gathering a broad variety of information about the business and its context;
- establishing a vision of the future and strategies for change;
- meeting the long-term interests of customers, stockholders, employees, and others who have a stake in the enterprise.

COMMUNICATING THE VISION
- developing credibility in the eyes of individuals and groups whose co-operation or compliance is needed;
- communicating often and in many ways the vision and strategies;
- creating thereby a culture/environment which elicits commitment to making the vision a reality.

ENERGISING/INSPIRING/MOTIVATING
- keeping people moving, despite the obstacles;
- being enthusiastic, supporting their actions to achieve the vision;

- being a cheerleader and role model for them;
- recognising and praising their successes;
- helping them overcome major political, bureaucratic or resource-related barriers to change.

If all the above is done well, the result is useful change.

Kotter's views on *management* include:

PLANNING AND BUDGETING
- setting targets that are realistic in the light of historical results;
- establishing detailed steps for achieving those targets;
- including timetables and guidelines in these detailed steps;
- allocating resources to accomplish those plans.

ORGANISING AND STAFFING
- establishing an organisational structure and set of jobs which fit the plan requirements;
- staffing this with appropriate people;
- communicating the plan to those people;
- delegating responsibility for carrying out the plan;
- linking compensation and other incentives to achieving the plan;
- establishing systems to monitor the implementation of the plan.

CONTROLLING AND PROBLEM-SOLVING
- monitoring results versus plan in detail;
- doing this formally and informally, using reports, meetings, etc.;
- identifying deviations from the plan—usually called 'problems';
- planning and organising to solve these problems.

If all the above is done well, the result is predictable results within important dimensions.[2]

I suppose there is value in distinguishing between leadership and management in this way, if only to provide a check-list of the activities and responsibilities of business leaders and managers today.

More interesting, perhaps, is a look at those characteristics of successful general managers or chief executives in today's major companies—and whether they are manager or leader characteristics, they *work*:

Spend most of your time with others

Practise MBWA (Managing By Wandering About); get out of your office—make a deliberate policy of doing so, otherwise you'll always find something else to do. A managing director I know does this regularly, and, by just *listening*, discovers a great deal that helps to make his company successful. It is also a great way to motivate staff: on one of his travels he came across a group of young women in a relatively junior department, and asked them what they would like to be called. One of them replied that she had always wanted to be a 'Supreme Commander', so he had some cards made up and presented them to her. At little cost he had motivated one staff member at least—and her colleagues too—and had established a means of communicating regularly and in a human way.

Go around the formal chain of command

Tom Peters,[3] one of the best-known management gurus in the world, reckons that every successful business leader has got to his or her position by *cheating*: not in an illegal way, of course, but by bypassing bureaucratic systems in order to get what was wanted to enable individuals or teams to succeed and achieve. So don't take 'no' for an answer.

Don't limit focus to planning strategy

Keep an eye on how things are working out: talk to the people close to the job, who usually see things very clearly. Keep your feet on the ground. Remember the saying, 'I'd rather achieve a 1 per cent improvement in 1,000 things than a 1,000 per cent improvement in one thing.'

Ask lots of questions

Of everyone, employees, suppliers, customers: be known as a person who won't let anyone get away with anything. If you ask for information, write down what you have been told in the privacy of your office, and keep the information—and its supplier—on file.

Rarely seem to make big decisions

Remember the approach of Lao Tse and Ranulph Fiennes in the previous chapter. Let people think the discovery, the decision, the success, was theirs. Be a role model for the fact that big decisions are usually the culmination of many smaller ones—and *both are equally important.*

Engage in activities that seem to waste time

Because they involve talking and listening to people, and you can't do that if you are always giving the impression of being in a hurry or watching the clock. Have time for people, and be innovative, not predictable, in the way you spend your time.

Rarely give orders—influence

Suggest, advise, ask leading questions: these are all better ways of coaching or managing than giving direct orders. Yes, it can be overdone: I recall Maurice Wood, when he was Bishop of

Norwich, referring in a sermon to Jesus' words, 'I will make you fishers of men'. 'What would you say,' he said, 'of a fisherman who came back from a day's fishing with the admission ''I haven't actually caught any, but I've influenced a few''?' But the basic point remains: getting people to come to their own conclusion, their own self-motivation, is better than applying *force majeure* or force of personality—both are exercises in power play.

Encourage individual creativity and react to others' initiatives

The most successful business leaders encourage staff to moonlight, to take work home, to experiment, in order to take a risk that they may achieve something extraordinary. One international computer company encourages its staff by giving them a budget to finance any project they come up with which looks as if it might work. If it succeeds, they throw a party to celebrate; if it fails ... they throw a party to celebrate, to show in a highly visible way that it is the continuous commitment to success and change that is important, not just the success itself.

This blend of leadership, management and risk is well illustrated by the model produced by Professor Ralph Stacey of the University of Hertford and used by Executive Development Consultants Ltd in London on their leadership skills seminars. I find it one of the most useful I have come across in defining the need for leadership *and* management as we approach the millennium. It confronts the dilemma of how organisations can find—or learn—their way into a future which they cannot foresee.

Managers traditionally collude together over decisions with implications that stretch far into the future, on the blithe assumption that they can assess and control the results. The horizon of predictability, however, is usually amazingly short, perhaps only measurable in months—so 'Blithe Spirit' gives way to 'Brief Encounter'.

The diagram shows the contrast between leadership and man-

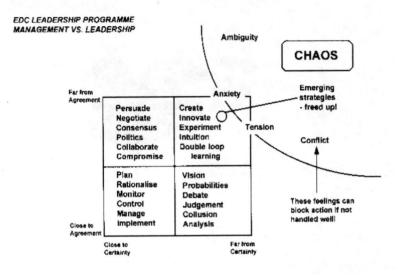

EDC LEADERSHIP PROGRAMME
MANAGEMENT VS. LEADERSHIP

agement in terms of certainty and agreement: in the box where 'close to certainty' and 'close to agreement' meet, it is possible to plan, monitor and control—in effect, to manage. When confronting a future 'far from certainty' and with little agreement as to what to do, this approaches a world of turbulence bordering on chaos, where the qualities needed embrace:

- experimenting
- risk-taking
- creativity
- innovation
- intuition

These generate considerable emotions, the handling of which becomes a major part of the leadership role.

Perhaps the last word on the difference, if any, between leadership and management comes from Warren Bennis again: 'The factory of the future will have only two employees, a man and a dog. The man will be there to feed the dog. The dog will be there to keep the man from touching the equipment.'

In that scenario, who is the leader?

CHAPTER 5

'Look at it This Way . . .'
Changing perspectives

. . . the second time round, she came upon a low curtain she had not
noticed before, and behind it was a little door about fifteen inches high:
she tried the little golden key in the lock, and to her great delight it
fitted!

Alice opened the door and found that it led into a small passage, not
much larger than a rat-hole: she knelt down and looked along the
passage into the loveliest garden you ever saw. How she longed to get
out of that dark hall, and wander about among those beds of bright
flowers and those cool fountains, but she could not even get her head
through the doorway; 'and even if my head would go through,' thought
poor Alice, 'it would be of very little use without my shoulders. Oh,
how I wish I could shut up like a telescope! I think I could, if only I
knew how to begin.' . . .

There seemed to be no use in waiting by the little door, so she went
back to the table, half hoping she might find another key on it, or at
any rate a book of rules for shutting people up like telescopes: this time
she found a little bottle on it ('which certainly was not here before,'
said Alice), and round its neck a paper label, with the words 'DRINK
ME' beautifully printed on it in large letters . . . 'I'll look first,' she
said, 'and see whether it's marked "*poison*" or not' . . .

However, this bottle was *not* marked 'poison', so Alice ventured to taste it, and finding it very nice . . . she very soon finished it off.

*   *   *

'What a curious feeling!' said Alice. 'I must be shutting up like a telescope.'

And so it was indeed: she was now only ten inches high, and her face brightened up at the thought that she was now the right size for going through the little door into that lovely garden. First, however, she waited for a few minutes to see if she was going to shrink any further: she felt a little nervous about this; 'for it might end, you know,' said Alice, 'in my going out altogether, like a candle. I wonder what I should look like then?' And she tried to fancy what the flame of a candle is like after it is blown out, for she could not remember ever having seen such a thing.

After a while, finding that nothing more happened, she decided on going into the garden at once; but alas for poor Alice! When she got to the door, she found she had forgotten the little golden key, and when she went back to the table for it, she found she could not possibly reach it . . .

Soon her eyes fell on a little glass box that was lying under the table: she opened it, and found in it a very small cake, on which the words 'EAT ME' were beautifully marked in currants. 'Well, I'll eat it,' said Alice, 'and if it makes me larger, I can reach the key; and if it makes me smaller, I can creep under the door; so either way I'll get into the garden' . . .

*   *   *

'Curiouser and curiouser!' cried Alice . . . 'now I'm opening out like the largest telescope that ever was!' . . .

Just then her head struck against the roof of the hall: in fact she was now more than nine feet high . . .

After a time she heard a little pattering of feet in the distance, and she hastily dried her eyes to see what was coming. It was the White Rabbit returning, splendidly dressed, with a pair of white kid gloves in one hand and a large fan in the other . . .

Alice took up the fan and gloves, and, as the hall was very hot, she kept fanning herself all the time she went on talking: 'Dear, dear! How queer everything is today! And yesterday things went on just as usual. I wonder if I've been changed in the night? Let me think: was I the

same when I got up this morning? I almost think I can remember feeling
a little different. But if I'm not the same, the next question is, Who in
the world am I? Ah, *that's* the great puzzle!'

*   *   *

Frank felt good. He had been doubly lucky today. He had got
that new large cardboard box from the department store, which
was quite big enough for him to use as a sleeping bag and thick
enough to give him some warmth. And then he didn't often find
a doorway in the Strand as good as this. It was out of the draught
and fairly close to the Savoy Hotel, where he might even pick
up some leftovers later that night. Yes, it was a good day . . .

'I just must try these on straight away,' said Margaret to her
friend Sue on their return from a shopping trip to the West End.
Soon a pile of dresses, shoes and underwear was laid out on the
bed. Margaret gave proper attention to each garment, revelling
in the rich fabric, supple leathers and frothy lace—and of course
the admiration from her audience.

'What about the cardboard boxes?' said Sue. 'I'm sure you've
paid quite a bit just for packaging.'

'Oh throw them outside,' replied Margaret. 'Hugh will sort
them out later—we may even have a bonfire' . . .

'So that's decided,' said the chairman, 'we close the Durham
packaging factory and go for the new plastic-coated design. Sorry,
Joe, I know how much that factory and its staff meant to you.'

'And to my father and his father before him,' said Joe in a
quiet voice.

'But the board must do the best thing for the shareholders,' the
chairman continued, 'and if we're to hold on to market share, we
must forget cardboard and go for new processes, new technology:
it'll be best for everyone in the long run—even our workers' . . .

It is strange how everyday objects or materials as mundane as
cardboard can take on different degrees of importance, depending
on our circumstances, our perspective, our values.

One of the reasons why I like—and find appropriate—the passage in which Alice changes her shape, her size (and in the process her perspective), is because not only does she believe she has some control over it ('I think I could, if only I knew how to begin'), but the change in perspective leads to the 'great puzzle', perhaps the greatest puzzle of all—'Who in the world am I?'

It is all too easy to get locked into one way of thinking, one perspective, and have that govern every single thing that we do. Both people and companies may fail to realise their full potential unless they are open to ideas and prepared to see things differently. And as it happens, changing perspectives in organisations is one of the few areas where corporate objectives can genuinely align with personal goals, to mutual advantage. Organisations can provide the culture, the parameters, the resources, the incentive to change, but individuals also need to respond by reassessing the way they look at their life.

For example, a wiper rag business, which made rags to wipe down industrial machines, was reasonably profitable, with good margins, until the managing director realised that there was a vast potential for increasing profitability by seeing the business in a new light: wiper rags were only a small part of the total cleaning needs of the companies with which they dealt. The company now handles waste, treats effluent and solvent, and engages in environmental health—in short it is now in the industrial care business and no longer in the wiper rag business alone. A simple change of attitude worked to broaden the entire concept of the company. The rag is still a rag, but it is looked at differently.

A similar silent revolution occurred in W.H. Smith, the high street stationers and booksellers. Sir Malcolm Field, the then CEO, started the process when he realised that profits were vulnerable because the supermarkets were taking their business. Sir Malcolm announced a shift in attitude at Smith's—he said they were now moving from the traditional set of categories of items to sell, such as books, stationery, magazines and videos, to selling

concepts like information, communication and home entertainment.

Such 'repackaging' is going on all the time, but is it a mere
cosmetic exercise or does it have *long-term* significance?

I believe such different ways of viewing matters are absolutely
fundamental to achieving lasting change. To give one illustration:
in any expenditure-reduction exercise, training is usually the first
overhead cost to be cut. However, a recent survey of human
resources practices in the retail financial services sector threw a
different perspective on training course costs. The survey states:

> Learning Resource Centres—areas set aside for employees
> to learn, with learning materials available provided by the
> employer—can range from the simple to the expensive and
> sophisticated, including computer-based learning facilities.
> What is a recurring theme, however, is that individuals are
> taking greater responsibility for their learning and develop-
> ment. This makes it a more cost-effective option for an
> organisation to provide this type of learning opportunity, as
> opposed to providing courses, which tend to be expensive.[1]

Here is another instance where a change of perspective goes
straight to the bottom line.

As for people, there is just as much stress and pressure on
those who are in work, trying to cling on to their jobs by working
all hours of the day and night, as there is on those who are out
of work and struggling to find jobs on their own. How do people
create time, space and a different perspective to look after themselves and their careers and futures?

It is a key question, the 'great puzzle' Alice asked herself, to
which we keep returning.

Possible answers to it, as individuals try to adapt their perspective to suit changing times, include:

● Carry on doing everything you do and encroach on your
   sleeping time. In the short term this is manageable, but in
   the long term you will have health and performance problems.

- Give yourself thinking time by delegating more. This works if you have people to delegate to—but if you haven't, can you delegate indirectly?
- Overcome a feeling of powerlessness in the situation by gaining from others in the organisation the know-how, the power, to cope with it.
- Eat into time devoted to your social life and family. But beware!—the former can be disruptive, the latter disastrous.
- Change, by discussion, the content of your job.
- If all else fails, change your place of work.

In these times of change, very little has changed more than the world of work. And when change occurs, what is left behind, and what is retained? For most of us, times of change are times to rethink, take stock, examine our hopes and assess our chances of attaining our dreams.

They are times of choice. Even if we are not in a change process at present, it would be prudent to take steps to ensure that when change does come for us—and we shall be unusual indeed if it doesn't—we are well prepared. Remember the Alice Principle: *To be employed is to be at risk; to be employable is to be secure.*

All of us would be wise to keep a watch on our employability, our ability to meet new demands, our capacity to remain ourselves while adapting to a different world. Both we and our organisations or employers have a responsibility in this—it is a partnership.

There are also international, global changes occurring, which mean that new moral and economic dilemmas will confront us on a scale unknown for many years. As economic power shifts to South East Asia, and political power to the vast sub-continent of China, how will we react to the resultant changes, whether they are threats or promises?

As Dr John Atherton of Manchester Cathedral, a trenchant thinker on economic affairs, commented on the new global market, in a lecture sponsored by the Industrial Mission at Basingstoke in 1995, 'If we are not prepared for economic evolution, we shall be faced with political revolution.'

Strong words, perhaps, and as we stand in the train or bus and pass sardine-like through Oxford Circus, it may all seem so remote, part of another world. But the need is surely still there to realise the responsibility and power we all have, leaders and team-members alike: the responsibility to be true to our values, and not to run away from the moral dilemmas presented by a developing career, a change of career, or world change on a mammoth scale, by compartmentalising our lives into little boxes—even those made of cardboard.

CHAPTER 6

Sticking to Your Knitting
What business are you in?

[Alice] looked at the Queen, who seemed to have suddenly wrapped herself up in wool ... She couldn't make out what had happened at all. Was she in a shop? And was that really—was it really a *sheep* that was sitting on the other side of the counter? ... she was in a little dark shop, leaning with her elbows on the counter, and opposite to her was an old Sheep, sitting in an arm-chair knitting, and every now and then leaving off to look at her through a great pair of spectacles.

'What is it you want to buy?' the Sheep said at last, looking up for a moment from her knitting.

'I don't *quite* know yet,' Alice said very gently. 'I should like to look all round me first, if I might.' ...

The shop seemed to be full of all manner of curious things—but the oddest part of it all was, that whenever she looked hard at any shelf, to make out exactly what it had on it, that particular shelf was always quite empty: though the others round it were crowded as full as they could hold.

'Things flow about so here!' she said at last in a plaintive tone, after she had spent a minute or two in vainly pursuing a large bright thing ...

'Can you row?' the Sheep asked, handing her a pair of knitting needles as she spoke.

'Yes, a little—but not on land—and not with needles—' Alice was beginning to say, when suddenly the needles turned into oars in her hands, and she found they were in a little boat, gliding along between banks: so there was nothing for it but to do her best . . .

So the boat was left to drift down the stream as it would, till it glided gently in among the waving rushes . . . and for a while Alice forgot all about the Sheep and the knitting, as she bent over the side of the boat, with just the ends of her tangled hair dipping into the water—while with bright eager eyes she caught at one bunch after another of the . . . scented rushes . . .

'Oh, *what* a lovely one!' [she said to herself.] 'Only I couldn't quite reach it.' And it *did* seem a little provoking ('almost as if it happened on purpose,' she thought) that, though she managed to pick plenty of beautiful rushes as the boat glided by, there was always a more lovely one that she couldn't reach.

'The prettiest are always further!' she said . . . and began to arrange her new-found treasures.

What mattered it to her just then that the rushes had begun to fade, and to lose all their scent and beauty, from the very moment that she picked them? . . .

'Are there many crabs here?' said Alice.

'Crabs, and all sorts of things,' said the Sheep: 'plenty of choice, only make up your mind. Now what *do* you want to buy?'

'To buy!' Alice echoed in a tone that was half astonished and half frightened—for the oars, and the boat, and the river, had vanished all in a moment, and she was back again in the little dark shop.

*   *   *

Mark Twain, in *Pudd'nhead Wilson*, advised: 'Put all your eggs in one basket—AND WATCH THAT BASKET.'

That was, I suppose, the classic stance for businesses before the growth of conglomerates in the '70s and '80s: companies knew what business they were in, and concentrated on improving it and making it more and more profitable.

But during that period the pace of change grew so rapidly that this approach began to be questioned: after all, eggs can break or grow stale, and then your business disappears. Hence the growth of the conglomerates, as companies diversified into different sectors and markets, in order to protect themselves against potential losses if they got it wrong in their attempt to outguess the market. Often this would result in organisations, especially multinationals, acquiring a strange mix of disparate companies which had little in common with each other; and with the pace of change continuing to grow still faster, now on a global scale, fulfilling the original purpose of diversification (insurance against commercial vulnerability) became like playing three-dimensional chess against a computer programmed for random, as well as orthodox, moves.

Also, these organisations tended to have characteristics which made them vulnerable to the very changes they were trying to ward off: they were large, hierarchic and volume-driven, slow to respond to new pressures. Often they were centralist in their approach, looking for uniform solutions. For staff, careers were vertical, with demarcations between jobs, and relatively secure.

All this made them vulnerable to the social, economic and political pressures which struck them in the '80s and the early part of the '90s:

- Competition, especially from the emerging countries in the Far East with their huge economic potential, such as Singapore, Malaysia, South Korea, Hong Kong—and China.
- Technical innovation, leading to product innovation and differentiation.
- Mergers and acquisitions, on a global scale.
- Environmentalism, changing the rules, and often the game itself.
- Specialisation, enabling added value to be gained from economies of scale and 'know-how'.
- Social change, altering customer expectations and behaviour.
- Deregulation, increasing pressure from competitors who often had (to Western countries) unbelievably high labour costs.

The list goes on—but it illustrates how the commercial and industrial changes we now see have come about, and sharpens the question, 'What business are you in?'

Rather like the passage from 'Alice' quoted above, however

New organisations

hard companies strove for the 'large bright thing' of commercial success, it remained elusive, out of reach. And even if some successes were achieved (the rushes), they began to fade immediately, as others, even more attractive, emerged into view.

The old-style, pyramidic, cumbersome organisations could not cope with the new pressures, and were forced to change in order to survive.

So in this decade there has been a reverse trend towards the earlier concentration on a cohesive and integrated business strategy, with companies knowing very well what business they are in, and 'sticking to their knitting'.

But the business climate is now very different in other ways, too: businesses have to be more flexible and quicker to respond to changing markets and customer expectations—and they can do that by retaining within themselves only those activities which are core to their commercial existence: other activities, or functions, can be hived off to separate, but closely related, service providers.

To illustrate what I mean, imagine one of those rolls you get in Italian restaurants, which have a central piece of bread, with other sections round the outside so that the roll can be broken apart in pieces.

The central part is the core business, retaining relatively few activities: finance and marketing certainly, probably personnel, although I know companies who outsource even this, possibly research and development—although that can always be bought in—and perhaps some manufacturing, although again this can be subcontracted. Even sales forces can be 'purchased' as required.

On the outer edges are six 'pieces', linked to, but not part of, the core:

1 Temporary structures
These include contractors and subcontractors in the traditional sense, but also new resources like interim executives—highly qualified and experienced senior executives who spend their time, often towards the end of their career, assisting companies with short-term needs. Perhaps a project needs help in getting off the ground; perhaps a managing director has fallen sick; perhaps a newly appointed manager needs a mentor. Interim executives provide this kind of help, their 'agencies' working exactly like secretarial agencies but at a much higher level.

2 Flexible parts
These include outsourcing, on a permanent or long-term basis, where services are provided by outside agencies, and also the use of agency staff inside the company, such as in security, catering or cleaning. What is especially different now is that there is less and less of a gap between the core company and these ancillary service providers, so that you can hardly see the join. One international chain of health and beauty shops has an independent distribution company with its own office in the company

head office, precisely to ensure continued quality of service through better communication and shorter response time.

3 Devolved parts

Strategic alliances are one example of this (Marks & Spencer and Tesco sharing one site, for instance), where complementary skills and expertise can be used to mutual advantage. Another is the use of lease-back facilities, so that the core company owns very little by way of capital assets (Microsoft in America actually owns very little in the way of property or furnishings and fittings: its market value comes from its employees and its *intellectual* property).

4 Access to expertise

Many companies 'retain' specialist advisers to provide help on an ad hoc basis, and tele-access to advice and facilities is increasingly available. For instance, in London you can now use a 'virtual office'—as it happens, the name of the company—to provide all the office services you may require, but on an ad hoc basis. You, or your company, have your own telephone number, and an address (that of the virtual office itself). When an enquirer rings that number, an operator answers as if she works only for you in your own office; since she has previously been informed of your whereabouts, she can either put the caller through to your home, mobile or wherever, or say you are unavailable. In this last case, the enquirer can be connected to a 'pop-up PA', who will take messages or arrange appointments as if she worked exclusively for you. If it is a simple query about the services you offer, the enquirer will be transferred to another agency *in Manchester*, which does nothing but provide information of this kind for a wide variety of companies. Thus enquirers are treated efficiently, and have no knowledge of—or interest in—the fact that they have been communicating with a virtual office rather than your own, while you gain by paying only for the services you require when they are needed.

5   *Remote parts*

Freelance agents are included here, as well as an increasing number of people who provide a service from their homes: a classic case is the use by BT of homeworkers to operate the Directory Enquiry service, particularly in Scotland. It is an efficient use of their resources (telephone lines) and labour in an area of relatively high unemployment—and interestingly enough one which has brought about a significant social change in the way 'the office' is regarded. It is lonely working from home, so regular meetings at the office are arranged to provide *social* contact for the homeworkers, as well as the opportunity to discuss business matters.

6   *Collaborative parts*

In order to improve customer satisfaction, companies are trying to establish closer relationships with clients or customers, through advisory panels, product testing, market surveys and so on, but on a more structured and long-term basis than before.

The question, therefore, 'What business are you in?', is capable of many more variations—and answers—than used to be the case. 'What business ought you to be in?', 'Should you be a core business or a service provider?' and 'What new area of business could you be in to take advantage of the changed ways in which organisations operate?' are alternative questions, while individuals have a far greater choice of directions in which to go, as core businesses contract and service providers, consultants and ancillary agencies proliferate. The limits in the future can only be set by the imagination.

   BUT . . .

Having established the business you are in, it is advisable that other people, your market, know this, clearly and in relevant detail. It is no use analysing the market, finding a niche, providing a needed service, if your communication channels are blocked or non-existent. The following early example, from the handbook of a Japanese car manufacturer, of how to operate the ventilation system did nothing to enhance their reputation:

In setting the button, this system will clean any displeasure out and increase the comfortableness in the head, upon room heating or cloudiness removing by means of blowing the cold out through inter-panel outlet.

1   With the switching lever located at central blowing outlet, being raised up, the cold wind will blow out, regardless of the position of temperature control lever.
2   Set the wind direction by means of fin and dial on the inter-panel outlet.
3   Lay the lever down when unused.

Sometimes it is possible to communicate, but to concentrate on irrelevant or unimportant aspects. This (fictitious) review of *Lady Chatterley's Lover* is a case in point:

This fictional account of the day-to-day life of an English gamekeeper is of considerable interest to outdoor-minded readers, as it contains many passages on pheasant-raising, on apprehending poachers, ways to control vermin, and other chores and duties of the professional gamekeeper. Unfortunately, one is obliged to wade through many other passages of extraneous material in order to discover, and savour, these sidelights on the management of a Midlands shooting estate. This book cannot take the place of J.K. Miller's *Practical Gamekeeping*.

Both organisations and individuals need to know these days what business they are in, or ought to be in, making it loud and clear that this is the knitting that will provide a pattern for the future, and concentrating on the essentials that will lead to success.

At least it should avoid getting fleeced . . .

PART THREE

MANAGING PEOPLE

CHAPTER 7

1 + 1 = 3

Teams

It was high time to go, for the pool was getting quite crowded with the
birds and animals that had fallen into it: there were a Duck and a Dodo,
a Lory and an Eaglet, and several other curious creatures. Alice led the
way, and the whole party swam to the shore.

They were indeed a queer-looking party that assembled on the bank—
the birds with draggled feathers, the animals with their fur clinging
close to them, and all dripping wet, cross, and uncomfortable.

The first question of course was, how to get dry again ... 'In that
case,' said the Dodo solemnly, ... 'the best thing to get us dry would
be a Caucus-race.'

'What is a Caucus-race?' said Alice ...

'Why,' said the Dodo, 'the best way to explain it is to do it.' ...

First it marked out a race-course, in a sort of circle ('the exact shape
doesn't matter,' it said), and then all the party were placed along the
course, here and there. There was no 'One, two, three, and away,' but
they began running when they liked, and left off when they liked, so
that it was not easy to know when the race was over. However, when
they had been running half an hour or so, and were quite dry again,

the Dodo suddenly called out 'The race is over!' and they all crowded round it, panting, and asking 'But who has won?'

This question the Dodo could not answer without a great deal of thought, and it sat for a long time ... while the rest waited in silence. At last the Dodo said '*Everybody* has won, and all must have prizes.'

*   *   *

I came across an interesting quotation the other day:

'We trained hard, but it seemed that every time we were beginning to form up in teams we would be reorganised. I was to learn later in life that we tend to meet any new situation by reorganising, and a wonderful method it can be for creating the illusion of progress while producing confusion, inefficiency and demoralisation.'

'That's perceptive,' I thought. 'I wonder which management guru wrote that?' Idly looking for the author's name, I was astonished to discover it was written in AD 65 by Petronius Arbiter, in his *Satyricon*—so nothing changes, even after 2,000 years.

In recent years, teams or teamwork have taken on an increasing significance in organisational life. They are regarded as being 'a good thing', and something all organisations should have more of.

But why?

The reasons lie both in the increasing specialisation of knowledge and skills, and in the growing belief in the value of, and the need for, more participative forms of management. These days, therefore, a manager needs to be skilled at working *in* teams (in the role of team member), and *through* teams (in the role of team leader).

But what *is* a team? How do teams work? And how do you monitor their success or failure? To take these questions in order:

1   WHAT IS A TEAM?

A team may be defined as a collection of individuals who have been brought together to achieve a specific and common purpose. Their combined efforts are expected to produce not only a successful outcome, but also synergy, in that $1 + 1 = 3$, or the sum of the whole is greater than the sum of the individual parts.

To achieve this synergy, effective teams need to have made progress in each of four interrelated areas:

- *Goals* are clearly defined and well-communicated statements of purpose, against which plans are developed collaboratively.
- *Roles*, reporting relationships and accountabilities are clear, and an appropriate blend of personalities and technical skills exists to meet the requirements of the team's task(s).
- *Procedures* have been developed to satisfy both the task (= getting the job done), and the relationship (= recognition, achievement, involvement and identity) needs of the team.
- *Relationships* of a high quality exist, with a marked emphasis on trust, constructive feedback and personal satisfaction.

2   HOW TEAMS WORK

If we know what good teams look like, how do we achieve them? Three approaches to team development may help:

a   Stormin' Norman

One classic theory of team development, based on observation, suggests that teams go through three, possibly four, stages of development—whether they reach the fourth stage depends on how effectively task and relationship concerns are managed. The stages are:

- *Forming—the immature team.* At this stage, members look to the leader for direction, support and task definition. Levels of productivity are low, and of leader-centred behaviour high; enthusiasm and expectations are relatively high.

- *Storming—the fragmented team.* If a team meets the challenges and concerns of Forming, it will typically move to this stage, the stage of dissatisfaction. Communication difficulties arise, leadership roles are questioned, team morale sinks, as reality falls short of initial expectations.
- *Norming—the sharing team.* If a team survives the conflicts of Storming, it will move to a phase of trust, respect, self-esteem and open exchanges about feelings, facts and fancies, all begin to grow.

  The danger with this stage is that it may produce a feeling of comfort, with team norms evolving which discourage or inhibit individuals from rocking the boat, by producing challenges which threaten to re-open the Pandora's box of the previous, storming stage.
- *Performing—the effective team.* If the team can forgo comfort for real progress, it will move forward to the final stage of achievement, with members feeling they are part of a winning team, and recognising that they are all essentially interdependent.

b   Have you got a minute?

Ken Blanchard, author of *The One-Minute Manager*, integrated these stages of team development into his theory of Situational Leadership. Briefly, this states that there is no one right leadership style; rather, the appropriate style should depend on the development, or maturity, level of the team. Blanchard similarly sees four stages in team development, with appropriate behaviours at each:

- *Directing in the orientation (Forming) stage.* Key tasks here are establishing goals, planning, organising, giving directions, monitoring results.
- *Coaching in the dissatisfaction (Storming) stage.* Here the

need is for balancing directional activities (redefining goals and expectations, coaching, managing conflict) and supportive activities (listening, building supportive relationships).

● *Supporting in the resolution (Norming) stage.* The team now assumes some of the task and relationship functions provided earlier by the leader, who gives recognition and acknowledgement of this.

● *Delegating in the production (Performing) stage.* To some extent, the special status of the manager or leader now disappears, as team members accept and confront their differences constructively, and support each other's efforts.

c Ringing a Belbin with you

Meredith Belbin's work, based on detailed research with blue-chip companies like ICI and Unilever, is well known, widely used, and still very relevant.[1]

Basically Belbin found that teams were effective if a) individuals knew what their preferred 'role' was; and b) teams consisted of the right mix of roles needed for the task to be accomplished. Belbin defined eight roles initially:

● *Coordinator*—a leadership role, denoting the manager who leads *through* people.

● *Shaper*—the other leadership role for the person who is task-orientated and *directs* people.

● *Monitor evaluator*—the person who takes a cool, critical look at progress within the team and is good at analysis.

● *Resource investigator*—the interface between one group or team with another, possessed of diplomatic and communication skills of a high order.

● *Team worker*—the team member who balances the Coordinator by being people-orientated as well, and who acts as cement in a team, helping members to get on with each other.

● *Implementer*—who balances the Shaper by getting on with the job, and turning ideas into reality.

- *Plant*—the ideas person, coming up with new ways of doing things, or new things to do.
- *Completer finisher*—the time-manager, who ensures things are done to schedule, on time.

Later Belbin added the *Specialist*, who is not really involved in the group dynamics of a team, but who contributes particular expertise and knowledge as required.

Clearly a team producing standard widgets, week in, week out, is going to require a different mix of roles from one involved in the design of the successors to the Pentium chip, and should carefully select its members accordingly.

(There is, however, an interesting caveat here: last year I carried out a project for a major company which wanted to improve its success rate in recruiting site managers by 'profiling' the position. In other words, by using a group of successful site managers and examining their Team Roles profiles, we were able to identify the mix of roles that led to success. Future candidates were given a Team Roles questionnaire to complete, and if their role preferences matched those of the sample group, their chances of employment were enhanced. The process worked, to a point, inasmuch as the success rate of appointees did rise. But, as we deduced, the result was a number of *clones*: all right as far as it went, but the process clearly was *not* designed to find those maverick candidates who have that spark of creativity and innovation which can take a company in new directions and to even greater commercial success. That is not a fault of the Belbin instrument, but it shows the need for being careful about assumptions.)

As regards *individuals*, Belbin found that the most effective managers knew their own roles, and *played to their strengths*. They did not try to improve their weaker roles, but put themselves in situations where their strengths could be appreciated and maximised.

There has been much criticism of late of the simplicity and accuracy of Belbin's approach, but in my experience it has excellent face validity and empirical validation—in other words it looks as if it should work, and does!

3   MONITORING TEAM SUCCESS

As a practical guide, watch for symptoms of poor teamwork, which may include:

- failing output
- lowering of quality standards
- increasing customer complaints
- increasing staff grievances
- conflicts between staff
- low levels of motivation
- confusion about responsibilities
- poor communication
- poor/delayed decision-making

Providing practical treatment for the above symptoms should result from answers to this check list of questions:

GOALS
- Have we a clear mission statement?
- Have we set ourselves measurable annual objectives?
- Have these objectives been prioritised?
- Have we set goals in all our key task areas?
- Have we recognised and acknowledged potential short-term goal conflict?

ROLES
- Are individual roles, reporting relationships and accountabilities clear?
- How appropriate is the style of leadership for the team task(s)?
- Is each individual competent to perform his or her key tasks?
- Is the mix of roles appropriate to the team task(s)?

PROCEDURES

- How effectively do we reach decisions as a team?
- How effectively do we share management information?
- How effectively do we co-ordinate key activities?
- How effectively do we assure product/service quality?
- How effectively do we manage conflict within the team?

INTERNAL RELATIONSHIPS

- Where are the major areas of mistrust?
- Which relationships remain tense and constrained?
- How constructive is feedback within the team?
- Which relationships remain competitive and unsupportive?

EXTERNAL RELATIONSHIPS

- How are external groups viewed generally?
- How effective are relationships with each key external group?
- How effective are the mechanisms used to integrate with each of these groups?
- How much time and effort do we spend on identifying, building and monitoring key external relationships?

OVERALL, AT WHAT STAGE OF TEAM DEVELOPMENT ARE WE?

All that has been said in this chapter should provide a practical framework within which to look at teams in which you are a leader or a member. But some words of caution may also be helpful:

a   Not all individuals like teams: John Mortimer wrote, in *Clinging to the Wreckage*, 'Loyalty to the school to which your parents pay to send you seemed to me like feeling loyal to Selfridge's. Consequently I never cared in the least which team won.'

b   Not all companies like teams. These are the organisations that adopt the subversive change tactics referred to by Petronius Arbiter (see p. 66). But also, while most organisations today assume that teams and team players are good, this is not

necessarily true. Most organisations are driven by productivity needs. Disruptive loners may be far more productive
than employees who focus so much on being valued as part
of a team that they rarely finish anything. And the disruptive
non-team player may be very good at making everyone see
a problem from a different viewpoint.

c   Team-building takes time: established behaviour patterns do
    not change easily, or overnight.

d   Top management support is vital, if long-term impact is to
    be achieved. Such support has to be helpful and genuine, not
    manipulative: outdoor activity courses in Scotland or the Lake
    District are fine, but not if they are seen by top management
    as a way of achieving some draconian result. ('Let's give
    them a hard time and shake them up a bit . . .') The emphasis
    of such courses has to be on individual achievement and
    discovery, which often, but not always, leads to team achieve-
    ment and the discovery of group identity.

e   Agreed changes need to be built into the structure of the
    organisations. In the Dodo's Caucus-race there was nothing
    wrong with the objective that '*everybody* . . . must have
    prizes'. But with everyone starting and finishing when and
    where they chose, there was little chance of reaching a team
    solution which was just, motivating, and agreed by all.

f   Involvement enhances commitment. Team-building is only
    effective if every member feels he or she has been fully
    involved in the process.

g   Personnel changes change the change process. If significant
    membership changes occur in a team, the new balance of
    personalities, skills and expectations may make another team-
    building programme useful if not essential.

The England rugby team manager, Geoff Cooke, once said of
his time with the team, 'I didn't use a particular management
approach to the team from the outset, but in retrospect the letters
of the word 'ETHOS' sum up the five ingredients I used: Excellence, Thoroughness, Humility, Openness and Stability.'[2]

All players in a team, all executives in a team, need to exist
in a culture of *Excellence*, which the CEO, manager or coach
should develop through creating interest and 'wanting' to be
involved.

Thoroughness for Cooke concerns a detailed approach to planning, so that every individual knows where he or she fits in. The
manager who fails to prepare should prepare to fail.

Humility and respect for the individual, as we have seen, are
crucial to team-building.

A climate of *Openness* must be created, in which individuals
can express their concerns freely. How many times have executives found themselves in teams where, although everyone agrees
in the meeting room, actions outside deny that collective agreement and undermine success?

Finally, all organisations need to create continuity and *Stability*,
an atmosphere in which individuals are valued and where there
is security without complacency. No rugby player has a guaranteed place in the England team; no executive has a guaranteed
future with the company any more. Both, however, know that
they can share in success if their skills contribute to the endeavour
and that they are part of a winning team.

It is the opposite of the remark by Barry Beck, an American
hockey player: 'We have only one person to blame, and that's
each other.'

CHAPTER 8

Whatever Turns You On
Motivation

. . . the Duchess was sitting on a three-legged stool in the middle [of the kitchen], nursing a baby; the cook was leaning over the fire, stirring a large cauldron which seemed to be full of soup.

'There's certainly too much pepper in that soup!' Alice said to herself, as well as she could for sneezing.

There was certainly too much of it in the air. Even the Duchess sneezed occasionally; and the baby was sneezing and howling alternately without a moment's pause. The only things in the kitchen that did not sneeze, were the cook, and a large cat which was sitting on the hearth and grinning from ear to ear . . . the cook took the cauldron of soup off the fire, and at once set to work throwing everything within her reach at the Duchess and the baby—the fire-irons came first; then followed a shower of saucepans, plates, and dishes. The Duchess took no notice of them even when they hit her; and the baby was howling so much already, that it was quite impossible to say whether the blows hurt it or not.

'Oh, *please* mind what you are doing!' cried Alice, jumping up and down in an agony of terror. 'Oh, there goes his *precious* nose;' as an unusually large saucepan flew close by it, and very nearly carried it off.

'If everybody minded their own business,' the Duchess said in a hoarse growl, 'the world would go round a deal faster than it does' . . .

And with that she began nursing her child again, singing a sort of lullaby to it as she did so, and giving it a violent shake at the end of every line:

> 'Speak roughly to your little boy,
>   And beat him when he sneezes:
> He only does it to annoy,
>   Because he knows it teases.'

CHORUS
(In which the cook and the baby joined):
'Wow! Wow! Wow!'

While the Duchess sang the second verse of the song, she kept tossing the baby violently up and down, and the poor little thing howled so, that Alice could hardly hear the words:

> 'I speak severely to my boy,
>   I beat him when he sneezes;
> For he can thoroughly enjoy
>   The pepper when he pleases!'

CHORUS
'Wow! Wow! Wow!'

'Here! You may nurse it a bit, if you like!' the Duchess said to Alice, flinging the baby at her as she spoke. 'I must go and get ready to play croquet with the Queen,' and she hurried out of the room. The cook threw a frying-pan after her as she went out, but it just missed her . . .

(Later, at the Queen of Hearts' Croquet Game, Alice finds the Duchess in a different mood):
She had quite forgotten the Duchess by this time, and was a little startled when she heard her voice close to her ear. 'You're thinking about something, my dear, and that makes you forget to talk. I can't tell you just now what the moral of that is, but I shall remember it in a bit.'

'Perhaps it hasn't one,' Alice ventured to remark.

'Tut, tut, child!' said the Duchess. 'Everything's got a moral, if only you can find it' . . .

'The game's going on rather better now,' [Alice] said, by way of keeping up the conversation a little.

' 'Tis so,' said the Duchess: 'and the moral of it is—''Oh, 'tis love, 'tis love, that makes the world go round!'' '

'Somebody said,' whispered Alice, 'that it's done by everybody minding their own business!' . . .

'I quite agree with you,' said the Duchess; 'and the moral of that is—"Be what you would seem to be"—or if you'd like it put more simply—"Never imagine yourself not to be otherwise than what it might appear to others that what you were or might have been was not otherwise than what you had been would have appeared to them to be otherwise."'

'I think I should understand that better,' Alice said very politely, 'if I had it written down.'

*   *   *

Cyril Connolly, parodying Aldous Huxley, wrote, in *The Condemned Playground*, 'I ask very little. Some fragments of Pamphilides, a Choctaw blood-mask, the prose of Scaliger the Elder, a painting by Fuseli, an occasional visit to all-in wrestling, or to my meretrix; a cook who can produce a passable *poulet à la Khmer*, a Pong vase. Simple tastes, you will agree . . .'[1]

The question of how to motivate people at work is one of the most pressing, and difficult, problems a manager today has to face, since many factors which used to be at his disposal are no longer available to him—of which more later. It is a question that arises in many aspects of his job, such as recruitment and selection; deciding upon pay levels and awards; organising work; adopting a management style; coaching staff; appraising staff; seeking performance improvements. In all these activities the manager makes assumptions about what motivates the individual in question, usually based on the concept that motivation implies three things:

- a need, want or desire
- a goal, target or object
- an expectation that the goal will be achieved through the individual's own effort

THE THEORY

The basic theories of motivation are well known (and curiously 'stuck' in the sense that very little new thinking has emerged in the past ten to fifteen years). As a brief reminder:

Abraham Maslow, a clinical psychologist, argued that motivation should be understood in terms of an individual's attempt to satisfy one of five basic, but hierarchical, needs—as one level of need is met, the individual moves up to the next: *physiological*; *security*; *social*; *esteem*; *self-fulfilment*. Many people never get to the level of self-fulfilment. Maslow maintained that a satisfied need is not a motivator, only unsatisfied needs are (what kind of needs Cyril Connolly's list satisfies is difficult to say . . .).

Frederick Herzberg identified sources of satisfaction, which he called Motivators—such things as *advancement, recognition, achievement, responsibility, potential for growth*—and different sources of dissatisfaction, which he called Hygiene Factors (because nobody gets excited about hygiene unless it's not there)—such things as *working conditions, supervision, job security* and *company policy and administration*. Evelyn Waugh sums it up quite well in *The Ordeal of Gilbert Pinfold*: 'His strongest tastes were negative. He abhorred plastics, Picasso, sunbathing and jazz—everything in fact that had happened in his own lifetime.'

While Maslow's and Herzberg's theories are 'general', serving management thinking at policy level, the needs of the individual manager have been better served by Ed Lawler, whose model connecting effort and performance with motivation has proved helpful. It is based on three premises, which most managers appreciate to be true:

1   People will not be motivated to perform unless they feel there is a reasonable likelihood that they will attain the required level of performance if they expend a given amount of effort.
2   People will not be motivated to perform unless they perceive that the rewards they receive (and value) are dependent upon their attaining the required levels of performance.

3   People will not be motivated to perform unless they perceive
    that the rewards they receive are equitable in terms of the
    effort they expend.

So much, then, for the theories, which have proved useful over
time, and remarkably resilient to changes in the workplace.

THE PROBLEM

The problem now is that, with regular wage increases being
replaced by profit-related pay, over which the individual may
have little control, and fewer promotion prospects because organisations are flatter, managers have less room to manoeuvre to
achieve the motivation they seek.

   That is why many companies currently resort to sending groups
of managers on, for example, outdoor training courses, and are
then surprised when the participants come back fired with the
'flu rather than enthusiasm. Since that does not work, companies
may then try shouting louder, producing elaborate internal PR
campaigns designed to motivate through communication about
the good things that await . . .

   While running courses for senior managers, I have sometimes
suggested that they imagine they are shop-floor workers or fore-
men at the end of a week in which a large number of their
colleagues have been made redundant. When I in turn role-play,
acting as a chief executive, and tell them that now, if we all pull
together, success, good times and financial reward will be theirs,
their natural response is quick, graphic, and electrifying to them
as senior managers . . .

SOME PRACTICAL SUGGESTIONS

Before suggesting solutions, it may be useful to ask *questions*
about the areas in which increased motivation may result from
improved communication or restructuring:

●   Has the person the ability to meet the required performance?

- Are the task objectives clear and specific?
- Does the person understand and accept the objectives?
- Has the person the necessary resources with which to achieve them?
- Does the person receive regular performance feedback?
- Does he or she value the rewards offered by the job?
- Is the person seeking other rewards?
- Are the rewards received dependent on performance?
- Does the person feel he or she is being rewarded fairly?
- Is the person experiencing problems outside work?

Based on the answers to these questions, can any of the following help?

- Altering the physical and social setting of the job?
- Enlarging, enriching the job content?
- Coaching and/or mentoring?
- Off-the-job training?
- Clarifying and resetting objectives?
- Discussing performance more regularly?
- Career counselling?

MOTIVATING IN A CONFINED SPACE

If room to manoeuvre really is tight, consider ways in which jobs may be enriched or enlarged. Yes, it is based on classic Herzberg, but why not, if it works?

1   Select those jobs in which motivation will make a difference in performance.
2   Approach these jobs with the conviction that they can be changed.
3   Brainstorm a list of changes that may enrich the jobs, without concern for their practicality.
4   Screen the list to eliminate suggestions that involve hygiene factors, rather than actual motivation.
5   Screen the list for generalities, such as 'give them more responsibility', which are rarely followed in practice. Motiv-

ator words have never left industry; the substance has just been rationalised and organised out. Words like 'responsibility', 'growth', 'achievement' and 'challenge', for example, have been elevated to the lyrics of the patriotic anthem for all organisations. It is the old problem of the pledge of allegiance to the flag being more important than contributions to the country—of following the form rather than the substance.

6   Screen the list to eliminate any suggestions which move responsibilities sideways.

7   Avoid direct participation by the employees whose jobs are to be enriched. The job is to be changed, and it is the content that will produce the motivation, not attitudes about being involved or the challenge inherent in setting up a job. A sense of participation will result only in short-term movement.

8   Carry out 'before and after' attitude tests.

9   Be prepared for a drop in performance in the experimental group during the first few weeks. The changeover to a new job may lead to a temporary reduction in efficiency.

10 Expect your first-line supervisors to experience some anxiety and hostility over the changes you are making. The anxiety comes from their fear that the changes will result in poorer performance for their unit. Hostility will arise when the employees start assuming what the supervisors regard as their own responsibility for performance. The supervisor without checking duties to perform may then be left with little to do. Later, however, the supervisors usually discover the supervisory and managerial functions they have neglected, or which were never theirs, because all their time was given over to checking the work of their subordinates.

It is interesting that the Duchess in 'Alice' uses both stick and carrot in her dealings with her baby and Alice respectively—all to little effect, since neither threat nor ingratiation works these days with people when used on their own. When they are used by the same person at different times the effect is even worse, causing the manager, who is trying to be all things to all men, to be regarded as a laughing stock—even though he may inspire fear if he has the power to decapitate, literally or metaphorically. Mind you, the last 'moral'—'Never imagine yourself not to be otherwise . . .'—is couched in language perilously near the opaque words of some management gurus, even those writing on motivation.

But for me, motivation in the '90s and beyond is summed up by four watchwords:

- **Communicate** with employees, so that they know what is happening, what to expect, how they can help, how they can be helped. This may be by company newspaper or memo, but is far better if it is done face to face, with opportunities for answering questions.
- **Listen** as well: the suggestions and comments of those closest to the job are usually well worth heeding.
- **Use** your ingenuity to devise new ways of motivating, relevant to the needs of staff and the current situation of the business. The Personnel Vice-President of a multinational visited the company's factory in Kenya, where there was a problem with absenteeism. He noticed that during breaks many of the workers congregated round a huge pot containing a very watery broth, into which they put the meagre bones and scraps of meat they had brought. He suggested that the company donate a few joints of meat for the pot, and absenteeism ceased virtually overnight. I am not suggesting that this technique might work in Neasden or New Jersey, but you get the point.
- **Encourage** in every way the recognition of staff who innovate, experiment or contribute in any way. One company I know formalises this by having notes of different colours, which anyone at any level can give to other staff to express appreciation for an unexpectedly good piece of work, or helpfulness or co-operation beyond the call of duty. It works.

Four simple things, but if you have worked out the acronym from the first letters, it should give you a better clue about motivating.

CHAPTER 9

Quis Custodit Custodes?
Providing resources

'Now one can breathe more easily,' said the Knight, putting back his shaggy hair with both hands, and turning his gentle face and large mild eyes to Alice. She thought she had never seen such a strange-looking soldier in all her life.

He was dressed in tin armour, which seemed to fit him very badly, and he had a queer little deal box fastened across his shoulders upside-down, and with the lid hanging open. Alice looked at it with great curiosity.

'I see you're admiring my little box,' the Knight said in a friendly tone. 'It's my own invention—to keep clothes and sandwiches in. You see I carry it upside-down, so that the rain can't get in.'

'But the things can get *out*,' Alice gently remarked. 'Do you know the lid's open?'

'I didn't know it,' the Knight said, a shade of vexation passing over his face. 'Then all the things must have fallen out! And the box is no use without them.' He unfastened it as he spoke, and was just going to throw it into the bushes, when a sudden thought seemed to strike him, and he hung it carefully on a tree. 'Can you guess why I did that?' he said to Alice.

Alice shook her head.

'I hope some bees may make a nest in it—then I should get the honey.'

'But you've got a bee-hive—or something like one—fastened to the saddle,' said Alice.

'Yes, it's a very good bee-hive,' the Knight said in a discontented tone, 'one of the best kind. But not a single bee has come near it yet. And the other thing is a mouse-trap. I suppose the mice keep the bees out—or the bees keep the mice out, I don't know which.'

'I was wondering what the mouse-trap was for,' said Alice. 'It isn't very likely there would be any mice on the horse's back.'

'Not very likely, perhaps,' said the Knight; 'but if they *do* come, I don't choose to have them running all about.'

'You see,' he went on after a pause, 'it's as well to be provided for *everything*. That's the reason the horse has all those anklets round his feet.'

'But what are they for?' Alice asked in a tone of great curiosity.

'To guard against the bites of sharks,' the Knight replied. 'It's an invention of my own . . . What's that dish for?'

'It's meant for plum-cake,' said Alice.

'We'd better take it with us,' the Knight said. 'It'll come in handy if we find any plum-cake. Help me to get it into this bag' . . . And he hung it to the saddle, which was already loaded with bunches of carrots, and fire-irons, and many other things . . .

Whenever the horse stopped (which it did very often), he fell off in front; and whenever it went on again (which it generally did rather suddenly), he fell off behind. Otherwise he kept on pretty well, except that he had a habit of now and then falling off sideways . . .

'I've had plenty of practice,' the Knight said very bravely: 'plenty of practice!'

*   *   *

An open letter to all Chief Executives and Managing Directors

Dear Sir/Madam,

I understand you are about to restructure your organisation to increase cost-efficiency and become more competitive.

This is the third reorganisation in three years and you are certain it will not be the last. The businesses you have directed have always changed, but the frequency and pace is much quicker now because of the technological advances.

While you have an expert management team geared to making profits, keeping shareholders happy and demonstrating responsibility in the community, I would like to share some thoughts on what you and your team owe to your people as you undertake the task.

Your existing employees have given you loyal service in return for security of employment, reasonable compensation and the opportunity of a career.

A new mind-set is forming, both with those employees and with new recruits. On 11 January, 1995, the then Director-General of the CBI, Howard Davies, told Exeter University students that 'employees needed to develop more skills and build up savings to see them through jobless periods.

'The future of the labour market is not going to be like the past,' he went on. 'Womb to tomb employment, a lifetime spent with one employer, is becoming the exception rather than the rule.'

Later that month, on the *Today* programme on BBC Radio 4, Kate Orebi-Gann, chairperson of the Association of Graduate Recruiters, said you had told her that you were 'unwilling to commit to long-term jobs and fixed costs', and that individuals could expect to have 'a sequence of jobs' with different organisations and in different settings.

You said to her also that 'graduates of today lack interpersonal skills'.

You wish and need to accomplish more with fewer people, and yet each current employee is having to do one-and-a-half jobs, with the pressure of longer hours. At the same time, you are expecting commitment from them and future recruits, while giving them the responsibility for managing their own future and not offering long-term contracts.

If this is true, then a new working environment is necessary, and this leads me on to the next group—you and all levels of management.

One of your junior managers said the other day, 'I survived downsizing, rightsizing, restructuring and re-engineering, then wham! Deconstructing got me.'

He is bemused by the terminology and unsure where he stands. He takes work home in the evenings and, while committed to his job, seems to have lost the zest and motivation he had. In the last three years he has twice been asked to reduce his staff, by five per cent and five per cent respectively, and, although he sees the benefit to the company, does not understand where either it or he is going.

His next-door neighbour at home has received training in how to handle the leaving process. Without training and not being used to firing people, your manager thinks he got it about right third time round.

He is concerned about how he can help those who are staying in his department, what it means to be a coach and how he can rebuild morale in his team. Managing uncertainty is a key issue for him, and he keeps thinking of the words he once saw in a Pogo comic strip: 'The certainty of misery is better than the misery of uncertainty'.

He is bemused by the number of different roles he has to play—expert, company representative, adviser, counsellor and team leader.

He sees and hears that you are trying to give managers responsibility, but the managers don't seem to want to adopt their role. And while you may think you can give managers responsibility, these people have to choose to take it on themselves, and need the right environment in which to operate if they do so.

The England rugby union team manager, Jack Powell, once said: 'I aspire as a coach to ensuring that, as the players go on the field, they will feel self-reliant.' The organisation can only do things to its people (through appraisals, career-planning, succession-planning and so on) in *partnership*.

Your staff know now that they are going to have to bite the bullet and learn to be responsible for their own development, but they want to do it in partnership with you. They want you to give them training and support, proper resources for the job, but too often firms are not providing the information individuals really want. There is too much about organisational issues, and too little about the individuals.

Those whom, as you say, you have to 'let go', become your ambassadors (or not, depending on how you helped them). Those of your people who are staying keep in touch with those who have left and experience similar emotions, wondering if they will be treated in the same way. Both are aware that some organisations provide outplacement support to those employees who leave, support which is practical, realistic, creative and caring.

Before you implement your restructuring, I hope your people will be at the top of the planning agenda, because it is they who will make it a success.

Yours sincerely,

*   *   *

Much of the above advice to senior executives is self-evident, but how frequently do we see or experience instances where it is unknown or ignored? And if resources *are* provided to the beleaguered managers, they are not modern, relevant, carefully designed and genuine tools for *development*, but the kind of ill-assorted baggage carried around by the White Knight in the passage quoted above: all collected from the past, all retained 'in case . . .', many ingenious but useless, all handled with incompetence. Amusing, perhaps—unless you happen to find yourself in *real* need, in which case the joke palls.

Mind you, there is another side: if dealing with people issues today is a partnership between the organisation and the manager, it is not always the organisation that is at fault. Not all managers want to take on responsibilities which are, quite properly, theirs, however supportive their organisation may be.

Next to that perennial phrase in the annual reports of companies, 'we hold that our people are our greatest asset', needs to be put an equally common, equally suspect phrase: 'we believe that people development and management are primarily the responsibility of line managers, not personnel'.

In June 1986, Paul Evans of INSEAD spoke on managing career development at a World Congress on Management Development in London. He said:

> It isn't the responsibility of the personnel staff, it is the responsibility of line management. Management is people and results, results through people. You can't delegate responsibility for results to the finance function . . . you can't delegate career management to the personnel function, though in both the support role is essential.

Some take this statement almost too far: one human resources director once told me that, having arrived at his new company, he looked at everyone with the word 'trainer' in their job title and got rid of them: 'If managers aren't training their own staff,' he said, 'then they're not doing their job and they will be held accountable accordingly.' That decisive action certainly initiated a radical rethink by both line managers and the in-house trainers about their approach to the business.

The majority of organisations, however, seem unable to introduce the *concept*, let alone encourage it to become part-and-parcel of the day-to-day actions of their managers.

A person, recently made redundant, came to me for career counselling. He had no idea what his manager had felt about him and his work, so I called the manager for some background information. His manager said: 'When I recruited him eighteen months ago, I knew within four weeks that I had made a mistake, so when the opportunity came for redundancies, his name went to the top of the list.' For a full seventeen months that manager was confronted almost daily with his 'mistake', without doing anything to alleviate the problem, until the convenient tool of redundancy via cost reduction came to his aid! Those months represented a huge waste of human resources due to the negligent passivity of the manager involved. As attitudes to the working environment shift and heightened competition makes efficiency even more important, there are fewer excuses for this sort of passive management.

However, there is hope: many of the casualties of the recession were in managerial or senior executive roles, and as they re-enter the job market they will have had some time and training to rethink their roles.

Shedding unsuitable staff is only one solution to career management, and a drastic one. Better still is for the organisation to train managers and work with them in making their staff fully effective. The Rank Organisation, for example, has initiated a broad-based programme for senior managers, designed to cover organisational skills, finance, information technology, marketing and human resources. Responsibility has been placed on the individual manager for his or her development, and to have constructive development dialogue with the boss. The company will be supportive where development is identified and mutually agreed.

Interestingly, research shows that while pay and rewards are seen by employers as key motivators, employees value more highly recognition that they are able to contribute in many different ways—and this means more career development provided internally. It is Herzberg all over again.

And it is cost-effective.

Linda Holbeche, in her Roffey Park report 'Career Development in Flatter Structures', concludes:

People can identify their personal goals and values through training ... In terms of costs to the organisation, replacement costs in terms of recruitment and opportunity time are likely to compare unfavourably to the costs of retraining trained and experienced employees. Unless organisations are willing to invest in their core workforce they will lose the commitment of skilled people.[1]

Yes, it means change. Yes, it means a partnership approach. Yes, it means commitment from both individuals and organisations alike; but as Stephen Covey says in his book *Seven Habits of Highly Effective People*, speaking as much of organisations as individuals:

> Change—real change—comes from the inside out. It doesn't come from hacking at the leaves of attitude and behaviour with quick-fix, personality-ethic techniques. It comes from striking at the root-fabric of our thought, the fundamentals which give definition to our character and create the lens through which we see the world.

SHARING RESOURCE MANAGEMENT

The following won't set the world to rights, but they may start the process of helping senior executives and managers to talk constructively together, and to agree priorities in the acquisition and allocation of (scarce) resources:

- **Set the priorities**—there is a big difference between being busy and being focused on what matters most as a manager. All too easily we get consumed by tasks and fail to stand back. Management intellect wilts in competition with managerial adrenaline. The key is learning the distinction between what we can and cannot control in the job of managing—it is the distinction between mastery of the situation and being a headless chicken—and it is an exercise which should be shared with senior management.
- **Put yourself in others' shoes.** Many management activities are difficult, sensitive and rare: reprimanding, raising personal issues like BO in an employee, disciplining, counselling, termination. Companies can help individuals with training, including role-plays, to be ready for these when they arise, and to understand what it feels like to be on the other side of the desk.
- **Know when to consult** the professionals. Very often

companies don't have the resources to tackle a problem, but, like John Wayne, try to tough it out in the mistaken belief that the macho approach will make it go away. Or managers say to themselves that they will manage it in their own time, and then somehow conveniently lose their watches! A problem shared is a problem aired and if it is out in the open and being discussed with someone independent, then new skills and new perspectives are more likely to be forthcoming.

- **Look forward, not back, and be prepared to take risks.** Don't get trapped in the past, with outmoded attitudes, doing what has habitually been done, and unwilling to discard anything in case, as the White Knight says, 'it'll come in handy' in the future. Establish with the organisation your 'degree of freedom', and then take the initiative . . . or ask for help.
- **Have regular check-ups**—in three areas:

  1 *Health.* In London, for example, Kleinwort Benson has provided an integrated occupational health programme at the bank, which takes individuals from employment medicals through to 'wellness' programmes. This provides an independent check for the executive on his or her physical health, but with the organisation's support.
  2 *Career.* Some organisations now provide a regular health check for employees in relation to their careers, using the services of outside consultants.
  3 *The 'resource-sharing' process itself.* As the approach *is* new, it is worth monitoring how well it is doing from time to time (not too often, though: it needs time to grow, and too often organisations and their managers pull out the carrots too soon, just to see if they are growing).

At least these suggested guidelines might stop the process of sharing resources coming to a halt as often as the White Knight, who was last seen by Alice 'tumbling off, first on one side and then on the other'.

CHAPTER 10

A Breakdown of Results
Managing pressure

. . . suddenly a White Rabbit with pink eyes ran close by her.

There was nothing so *very* remarkable in that; nor did Alice think it so very much out of the way to hear the Rabbit say to itself, 'Oh dear! Oh dear! I shall be too late!' . . . but when the Rabbit actually *took a watch out of its waistcoat-pocket*, and looked at it, and then hurried on, Alice started to her feet, for it flashed across her mind that she had never seen a rabbit with either a waistcoat-pocket, or a watch to take out of it, and burning with curiosity, she ran across the field after it, and fortunately was just in time to see it pop down a large rabbit-hole under the hedge . . .

After a time she heard a little pattering of feet in the distance . . . It was the White Rabbit returning, splendidly dressed, with a pair of white kid gloves in one hand and a large fan in the other: he came trotting along in a great hurry, muttering to himself as he came, 'Oh! the Duchess, the Duchess! Oh! Won't she be savage if I've kept her waiting!'

(Later, during the trial of the Knave of Hearts, the White Rabbit, acting as Herald, is asked to read some new evidence to the court):

The White Rabbit put on his spectacles. 'Where shall I begin, please your Majesty?' he asked.

'Begin at the beginning,' the King said gravely, 'and go on till you come to the end: then stop.'

These were the verses the White Rabbit read:

'They told me you had been to her,
    And mentioned me to him:
She gave me a good character,
    But said I could not swim.

He sent them word I had not gone,
    (We know it to be true):
If she should push the matter on,
    What would become of you?

I gave her one, they gave him two,
    You gave us three or more;
They all returned from him to you,
    Though they were mine before.

If I or she should chance to be
    Involved in this affair,
He trusts to you to set him free,
    Exactly as we were.

My notion was that you had been
    (Before she had this fit)
An obstacle that came between
    Him, and ourselves, and it.

Don't let him know she liked them best,
    For this must ever be
A secret, kept from all the rest,
    Between yourself and me.'

'That's the most important piece of evidence we've heard yet,' said the King, rubbing his hands.

*   *   *

It has been said of Christopher Columbus and his discovery of America that when he set out he didn't know where he was going, when he got there he didn't know where he was, and when he came back he didn't know where he had been.

Some people look for a job like that—at least to begin with:

they pass by opportunities presented to them, and are then puzzled when they take so long in getting settled again.

Because that sort of problem is within their control it is relatively easy to deal with. Far more difficult is coping with the kind of problems that other people cause them. You must know the sort of thing I mean—the myriad small ways that companies can strike at the confidence of those searching for a job: phone calls never returned; staff turnover so high that your story has to be repeated time and time again; 'no-no' letters which use the words of regret in a format that makes it obvious they are standard run-offs produced by an office junior; sometimes downright rudeness; nearly always delay, frustration, thoughtlessness . . .

Now I can think of three reasons why this kind of thing happens, putting further obstacles in the path of those already lacking confidence and hope.

First, very few organisations are in a hurry to fill a vacancy: it is a golden opportunity to save money, to rethink the place the job occupies in the organisation structure, to re-evaluate the dimensions of the job itself.

Second, there are some people—more, perhaps, than one might think these days—who genuinely lack basic ability. They may also be feckless and careless, and often tend to gravitate towards the softer end of the job market, where a lack of hard-nosed effectiveness and gritty achievement can be buried under a woolly blanket of well-meaning but unfocused incompetence. It is a matter of wonder to most people involved in recruitment and career counselling how many talented staff are on the job market, while others, more smooth-tongued or well-connected, but less able, survive the grim reapers of redundancy, early retirement or just plain dismissal.

Third, and by far the most widespread reason, I believe, for this lack of courtesy, consideration and competence, is that nearly everyone now in employment is working under such pressure that the rule of 'just too much' applies generally. Thus there is just too much work for all of it to be done properly; budgets have been cut back so far that it is just too much to afford the little bit extra which would transform mediocrity into brilliance; so much de-layering has taken place that providing adequate levels of service is just too much for those left behind.

Whatever the reason, the 'just too much' principle can cause havoc in all walks of life—from getting a badly-needed job to getting a washing machine serviced. The result is a sharp increase in pressure, one of the major diseases of our time.

A certain amount of pressure is vital for survival: if there is a spectrum of pressure from zero to breakdown, we need to be in the middle section: too much obviously causes problems, but so does too little—we vegetate and can even die without sufficient stimulus, whether internally or externally imposed, to keep us going.

These days, though, that is hardly the problem: it seems that if you are not stressed there must be something wrong with you. The relentless drive at work for performance targets means that we tend to have either one-and-a-half jobs or none at all—and both cause pressure.

It is interesting that this is a reversal of what has largely been the case in the past: in most centuries before this one, those who had the wealth had the most leisure, while those who had little wealth had no spare time. Now, however, those who have the wealth have little or no leisure, whereas those who have little wealth have most spare time.

That reversal increases the amount of pressure on those who have a job, but it also increases the pressure on those who have no job, and no means to spend their (enforced) leisure time. So both kinds of people rush around like the White Rabbit, nervous, concerned to do the right thing, to sort things out, to get to where they want to go *on time*.

What can be done? There is a plethora of techniques and advice on how to cope with pressure, and much of it is about as meaningful and helpful as the verses the White Rabbit quotes in the trial of the Knave of Hearts.

There are really, I suppose, two issues: what can companies do, and what can individuals do?

To take companies first, there are three things leaders or managers need to realise, if they are to make a positive contribution to relieving stress in the workplace:

1   Change in organisations always brings pressure, regardless of company or individual success: talk to an 'average' group in almost any organisation in the world and you will find, as a reaction to the continuous change process they will have been experiencing, pressure and, in turn, tiredness bordering on exhaustion. Unipart, the automotive parts company which has undergone a huge transformation following its British Leyland history, is now revitalised and very successful. It is brimming with new ideas for employee development, one of which is a 'university' in which employees can learn new skills. Response has been good, but the company has still found stress levels among employees have increased dramatically because of all the changes, leading to Unipart making rooms available for aromatherapy and reflexology—not the usual image, perhaps, of the brown-overalled end of the automotive industry. They have found it makes *commercial* sense to recognise that employees do suffer stress when surrounded by change, and to try to seek ways, however unusual, to help them.

2   All managers need to keep a wary eye on their staff and watch for signs that things may not be as they should be. In my experience, the *main* cause of major trauma in people is nearly always a breakdown of relationships in private life—a marriage or other close relationship: I have known, and advised, many people who have lost their jobs, but the only ones who have had serious breakdowns, or have even tried to commit suicide, are those who have had personal problems as well, which have pushed them over the edge. So to the extent that people have increasingly pressured jobs in terms of change, complexity and time, their personal lives are even more likely to come into the workplace and within the area of managerial concern. Employers need, therefore, to create

the right atmosphere and support to make it legitimate for people to address personal and work concerns.

3   Individuals under stress are perfectly capable, given the right encouragement and support, of managing themselves out of their predicament. Stephen Williams, in his book *Managing Pressure for Peak Performance*, highlights the positive approach to stress. He talks about 'building blocks' of change for people under stress: first, raising awareness of the situation by recognising warning signs; second, accepting individual responsibility, because although others may help, they cannot do it all, and it is no solution to try to relieve pressure by blaming others; third, taking action and then monitoring progress to see that the actions are having the desired effect.

As always, though, prevention is better than cure, and for those who want to try to avoid causing stress both to themselves and others, I suggest three simple things to try:

1   Put yourself in the other's position, and 'do as you would be done by'. It may take a little more imagination, but it needn't take more time or effort. One redundant executive I know was completely remotivated in his job search because a headhunter had taken the trouble to address how he might be feeling on getting a 'no-no' letter, and had sent a sensitive but honest explanation of why he had not been successful, rather than the standard 'Thank you for your application, but I regret that out of the large number of applicants there were some who more closely matched . . .' When that individual gets a job—as he shortly will—how much business is he going to give that headhunter, who happens also to be part of a larger consultancy?

2   Constantly ask yourself, 'Am I spending my time on things that *really* matter?' We all succumb to Pareto's 80:20 effect, where, for example, 80 per cent of the clothes we wear come from 20 per cent of our wardrobe, or 80 per cent of our business comes from 20 per cent of our customers, or 80 per cent of the work we do accounts for 20 per cent of the key

tasks we have. So why not revisit the other 80 per cent and see how much can be dumped, delayed or delegated? Perhaps this will release the extra time and energy we need to do our real job really well?

3 Remember the principle of 'just in time' process control where—with careful planning, communication and direction—resources, energy and manpower are not wasted or hoarded unnecessarily, but used to achieve a desired result in an agreed timescale. What is required is not more effort, but better quality effort applied at the right time.

With a little more 'just in time', and a little less 'just too much', there just might be less hassle in life for us and for others, less rushing around like the White Rabbit, less nonsense, and perhaps American, British and Spanish history books—at least as regards Christopher Columbus—would write a different story.

CHAPTER 11

Asset Management
Mentoring, coaching and training

'This here young lady,' said the Gryphon, 'she wants for to know your history, she do.'

'I'll tell it her,' said the Mock Turtle in a deep, hollow tone: 'sit down, both of you, and don't speak a word till I've finished.'

So they sat down, and nobody spoke for some minutes. Alice thought to herself, 'I don't see how he can *ever* finish, if he doesn't begin.' But she waited patiently.

'Once,' said the Mock Turtle at last, with a deep sigh, 'I was a real Turtle . . . we went to school in the sea. The master was an old Turtle — we used to call him Tortoise — '

'Why did you call him Tortoise, if he wasn't one?' Alice asked.

'We called him Tortoise because he taught us,' said the Mock Turtle angrily: 'really you are very dull!'

'You ought to be ashamed of yourself for asking such a simple question,' added the Gryphon; and then they both sat silent and looked at poor Alice, who felt ready to sink into the earth. At last . . . the Mock Turtle went on . . .

'I only took the regular course.'

'What was that?' inquired Alice.

'Reeling and Writhing, of course, to begin with,' the Mock Turtle replied; 'and then the different branches of Arithmetic—Ambition, Distraction, Uglification, and Derision.'

'I never heard of "Uglification",' Alice ventured to say. 'What is it?'

The Gryphon lifted up both its paws in surprise. 'What! Never heard of uglifying ... if you don't know what to uglify is, you *must* be a simpleton.'

Alice did not feel encouraged to ask any more questions about it, so she turned to the Mock Turtle, and said 'What else had you to learn?'

'Well, there was Mystery,' the Mock Turtle replied, counting off the subjects on his flappers, '—Mystery, ancient and modern, with Seaography: then Drawling—the Drawling-master was an old conger-eel, that used to come once a week: *he* taught us Drawling, Stretching, and Fainting in Coils ... the Gryphon never learnt it.'

'Hadn't time,' said the Gryphon: 'I went to the Classical master, though. He was an old crab, *he* was.'

'I never went to him,' the Mock Turtle said with a sigh: 'he taught Laughing and Grief, they used to say.'

*   *   *

In December 1994, *The Times* said that Mr Iain Sproat, the Sports Minister, would be going to Australia to discover the secret of success at cricket. This prompted John Radford, a professor in the Department of Psychology at the University of East London, to write a letter:

> I could have saved him the trouble ... There is abundant research evidence ... the main factors include the general encouragement of an area, careful selection of promising individuals, effective rewards, skilled coaching, preferably on a one to one basis, and, above all, carefully planned and persistent practice over a lengthy period, normally at least five to ten years ... As so often, the knowledge we have ... it is the application that is lacking.[1]

These qualities would apply as much to excellence in management as in sport, but that's not the point. The answers are right under our noses, but we neither recognise that the information is there nor, it seems, do anything about it. We reinvent the wheel.

This is as true for organisations as individuals. The organisation or employer knows it needs to invest in its people so that skills are not only kept up to date, but also sufficiently honed to take the organisation forward into the future. But, when a recession comes along, the first overhead to get the axe taken to it is the training function—the prime purpose of which is to ensure that the skills are in line with the business.

We should know better: The Institute of Personnel and Development paper 'People make the Difference' says that 'organisations with a reputation for transforming their approach to people management gear training and development to operational needs, longer term adaptability and personal growth',[2] and we know this to be self-evidently true.

But telling organisations not to cut training budgets is the commercial equivalent of the pantomime audience telling the deaf hero: 'Look behind you, look behind you!' as the villain creeps up from behind. Learning the need for greater self-awareness always seems to come too late—if at all.

On an individual level, there is a good example of what I mean in Bunyan's *The Pilgrim's Progress*. Christian falls prey to Doubt, and Giant Despair locks him up in Doubting Castle. He has been given all the resources he needs but, in the circumstances of doubt, panic and despair, he forgets all about them. Once he realises he has the key of Promise inside his tunic, he can unlock the door and go free.

Individuals need somehow to be made aware of what skills they do or do not possess, and be enabled to bring them out into the open, just as the key of Promise does. That is the key—as Muriel Spark says through her eponymous heroine in *The Prime of Miss Jean Brodie*: 'To me education is a leading out of what is already there in the pupil's soul. To Miss Mackay it is putting in of something that is not there, and that is not what I call education, I call it intrusion.'

The truth is, we often know we have the answers to problems right within ourselves but need help to get them out: we don't need or want to be told. Where can we get the wisdom and counsel that we need?

Traditionally companies have provided training and assistance in self-development; more recently coaching has been added to the vocabulary, and more recently still mentoring has crept into the curriculum, having been an unfashionable concept for many years.

To take them in turn:

TRAINING AND DEVELOPMENT

Personally I prefer the word 'development'—as someone has said, 'you train dogs, you develop people'—but we all know what is meant. This is not a personal development manual in the technical sense, but I think three points are crucial:

1   Any personal development programme must be relevant to the needs of the business as well as to those of the individual. I have always appreciated the advice to 'stand firm in your refusal to remain conscious during algebra. In real life, I assure you, there is no such thing as algebra.' Similarly it may be very enjoyable to spend a week in the Lake District climbing up, or falling (= abseiling) down, mountains, but who is really going to benefit? I have known *individuals* benefit greatly from such an exercise, but with limited subsequent value to the *company*. And yet companies have sent waves of managers over the (mountain) top, both the keen and the suspicious (the latter I would promote immediately in view of their perspicacity: the first activity for the team on a course I attended was to erect a tent in the dark next to a bog, and then spend the night therein, with a pre-breakfast exercise the next day of jumping into an icy beck, urged on by a leggy blonde tutor who nicely blended the qualities of the Marquis de Sade and Boudicca). The point was neatly summed up by a personnel director I know, who insisted on a gritty evaluation after any development activity: 'Training

is mere entertainment if it does not embrace evaluation which demonstrates increased performance and productivity.'

2   Different and developing situations in business call for differing approaches or solutions. I suppose if I were living under the sea I would find it more useful to study Reeling and Writhing, as the Mock Turtle did, than Reading and Writing, not to mention Drawling and Fainting in Coils. In our present business climate, with one emphasis at least on the drive for innovation (the *International Herald Tribune* reported in 1992 that since 1979, when Sony invented the Walkman, there had been a new model developed every three weeks), there is a need for senior executives to change their approach. Harry Quadracci, CEO of Quad/Graphics, once put it this way in a television interview: 'People think the President has to be the main organiser. No, the President has to be the main *dis*-organiser. Everybody "manages" quite well; whenever anything goes wrong, they take immediate action to make sure nothing will go wrong again. The problem is, nothing new will ever happen, either.' I recall talking to a corporate vice-president about what is currently valued in the pharmaceutical industry. In order to stay in business, he said, the industry has had to shift its values from selling pills through outlets to becoming 'case managers in disease management. The sale of a drug concerning Alzheimer's disease now has to be combined with counselling the family affected by the disease'. This subtle, but fundamental, shift has affected both the need for greater development of individual executives, and also what is taught.

3   Training and development are required as a permanent part of the career progression of managers at *every* level, even for top executives. For example, executive leadership implies a strong ego expressed in a self-assured attitude with a role of managing, or directing, other people. This needs a check and balance and an understanding of what can and cannot be managed. Also, executives are usually so busy running an enterprise, focused on the business, that they have spent little

time in personal reflection, so when they are faced with internal or external problems they may be less capable of dealing with them. For these and other reasons, executives are even more in need of objective advice. They are less likely to find advisers within the organisation and can find themselves isolated and lonely, carrying the burden of decision-making and policy decisions. As the direction of the organisation lies in the hands of those at the wheel, it is vitally important that they have as much back-up support as possible—perhaps, even, some . . .

MENTORING AND COACHING

In Greek mythology, Mentor was the experienced and trusted counsellor to the young Telemachus and is the one who has given his name to 'mentoring'. We don't need to go into a debate about the differences between mentoring and coaching, between developing a future and developing skills for present performance. It doesn't matter whether it is called mentoring, coaching, expert counsel, wisdom or general advice and guidance. What does matter is that people know where to go and to whom to turn when they need an independent and objective ear, a word, a thought or some astute questioning which leads them to an understanding of their way through a situation—and in a sympathetic and encouraging way, not in the intimidating way in which Alice was treated by the Gryphon and the Mock Turtle.

Fundamental to both coaching and mentoring is the fact that what you believe and value affects what you do and say. Many managers can gain an understanding of this, either by being coached themselves or through looking at what they do as though they were coaching themselves. If they are to succeed in a coaching role they require a great deal more than confident possession of the behaviours and skills they wish to pass on. The coach's personal values will certainly shine through the actions. Someone who is simply following a check list and going through the motions of being a coach will quickly transmit any scepticism and lack of enthusiasm to the learner.

What, then, are some of the qualities required by a coach or mentor which may help to unearth what you value?

- In the first place, you have to give out to get back. You have to know what it is you can give in terms of knowledge or skill, and be humble enough to accept when these may not be translated into action.
- You need to make learning interesting and fun, and so unleash the motivation and need in those you are guiding. How many career choices have been made as early as one's schooldays because of a certain teacher's approach?
- You need the ability to put yourself in the other person's shoes and to try to ask yourself, 'How would I want to be treated and receive this information if I had the same personality as this person?'
- You also need to bring individuals to the point where they can see and understand for themselves just what they and the situation require.

COACHING SKILLS

It may help to list a breakdown of the overall basic coaching skills (*listening, questioning, rephrasing/summarising, empathising, giving feedback*):

- select an important task or problem
- break this into stages
- involve the individual in setting objectives
- agree relevant and quantifiable criteria
- ensure the individual understands he or she is responsible for the solution of the problem
- encourage the individual to ask questions
- check his or her comprehension of discussions
- provide examples to stimulate discovery of a solution
- provide information in response to questions

- adjust the method and pace to the learning needs
- ensure the individual receives performance feedback, as near to the event as possible

At present, if organisations are not actually flatter in structure, then they are operating as such, with much shorter lines of communication and a much sharper focus on responsibility and accountability. The qualities needed in this working environment are numerous and different enough to make us pause and question how we bring them into reality: networking, cross-functional team skills, delegating, trusting, influencing, taking risks, creativity and lateral thinking, sharing, marshalling resources, sensitivity—the list goes on.

It must be cost-beneficial to look at our employees and say, if I view them as individual businesses, how can I as an employer help them to know what their skills assets are, and where it would benefit them most to invest those skills?

And if it is true that you only really value something when you lose it, working with a personal coach or mentor and adopting a coaching or mentoring mentality will help you and your employees to understand and recognise what you both value before you—or they—have to lose it.

Today's working environment can teach, like the Classical master in 'Alice', both Laughing and Grief: it makes sense to make use of the resources of development through training, mentoring or coaching to advance the former and reduce the latter.

CHAPTER 12

'I'd Like a Word With You'
Communication

'Twas brillig, and the slithy toves
    Did gyre and gimble in the wabe;
All mimsy were the borogroves,
    And the mome raths outgrabe.

'Beware the Jabberwock, my son!
    The jaws that bite, the claws that catch!
Beware the Jubjub bird, and shun
    The frumious Bandersnatch!'

He took his vorpal sword in hand:
    Long time the manxome foe he sought—
So rested he by the Tumtum tree,
    And stood awhile in thought.

And as in uffish thought he stood,
    The Jabberwock, with eyes of flame,
Came whiffling through the tulgey wood,
    And burbled as it came!

One, two! One, two! And through and through
    The vorpal blade went snicker-snack!

He left it dead, and with its head
  He went galumphing back.

'And hast thou slain the Jabberwock?
  Come to my arms, my beamish boy!
O frabjous day! Callooh! Callay!'
  He chortled in his joy.

'Twas brillig, and the slithy toves
  Did gyre and gimble in the wabe;
All mimsy were the borogroves,
  And the mome raths outgrabe.

'It seems very pretty,' [Alice] said ... 'but it's rather hard to under-stand!' (You see she didn't like to confess even to herself, that she couldn't make it out at all.) 'Somehow it seems to fill my head with ideas—only I don't exactly know what they are!'

*   *   *

If the Jabberwock was puzzling to Alice, another strange creature is now common on the M25 orbital motorway round London: it is always seen in cars, its natural habitat, its shoulders are hunched and there seems to be an antenna coming out of its ear. One might think it a lost and rather backward Martian, two planets short of a system, were it not for the fact that it is curiously sensitive to white cars and the blue lights so popular with the police.

He—or she, there is no sex discrimination here—is the person who has a car 'phone.

More and more people are joining the revolution in communi-cations, from car 'phones and the fuzz on the M25 to earphones and a buzz on the information highway. The conversational grace of *Pride and Prejudice* is giving way to the sinister soundbites of *Nineteen Eighty-Four*.

As with most revolutions, there is a high personal and social cost to be paid:

Among those affected *personally* are the many people who have lost either their job through redundancy, or their sense of direction—and humour—on finding they have survived. The first group say things like, 'I had no idea . . .', 'If only someone had talked to me . . .', or 'Nobody bothered to speak to me once it was known . . .' The survivors are more cautious: 'Look, no one tells *me* anything, so how can I communicate to my team?' or, more depressingly, 'I'm just about hanging on by my fingernails here, I'm working all the hours there are, so communication?— I should be so lucky to have the time. Anyway, nobody believes what people say here any more.'

Both these types of person need to speak about their feelings, and are desperate for someone to listen.

As for *social* cost, I can think of several examples:

1   The art of conversation—and the very use of the word 'art' is interesting—developed as people wished to communicate in a way which was interesting, clear, but subtle, giving nuances of meaning and interpretation and endowing the context in which the words were used with richness and wisdom. For this it was preferable that those conversing should be face-to-face in each other's company, with time not being too constraining a factor. How else could the subtleties of language be communicated than by the ability to *see* the raising of the eyebrow, the gleam in the eye, the play of the lips, which in turn enabled each person to perceive the feelings and judge the sincerity of others?

    Such face-to-face conversations today are rare indeed, and almost always brief—and the price we pay is a loss of human warmth, of a sense of belonging, which man as a social animal needs. Is not this 'depersonalisation' of communication one reason why the fabric of our society is in tatters?

2   A second example is provided by messages communicated by the ubiquitous e-mail, when we enter a world in which subtlety and richness are replaced by newspeak and an economy of words of famine proportions. 'NEED SMILEYS AND FROWNIES ***URGENTLY***' would be one of the clearer messages. Ironically a recent article supporting the use of this

gobbledegook as making communication clearer described it as 'disambiguating' the language we use . . .

Not that brevity is of itself bad: Victor Hugo wrote to his publisher, when he wanted to know how sales of *Les Misérables* were going, the single punctuation mark '?' They replied, with equal frugality, '!': economy of style has always been admired as the hallmark of a good writer, and there are of course commercial reasons why messages charged by the number of words or letters should be brief.

But brevity is one thing, levity another. And in a world of constant conflict, threatened or actual, where the nuclear family is overshadowed constantly by the possibility of nuclear warfare, I would sleep better if I were more sure that communication of literally world-shattering importance was being given the time, consideration and opportunity for the clarification it deserves, by people who were in touch with their own feelings and those of people like you and me because they were in touch with each other, and had time and vocabulary enough to make themselves clearly understood.

3 Alice's problem that she has no idea what the poem about the Jabberwock means and is too shy or frightened of looking silly to ask, is one surely all of us recognise. It is not new, of course: Gilbert and Sullivan's *Patience* has Bunthorne, one of the rival poets, realising how to manipulate this tendency:

> And everyone will say,
> As you walk your mystic way,
> 'If this young man expresses himself in terms too deep
> for *me*,
> Why, what a very singularly deep young man this deep
> young man must be.'

But it's not a helpful practice, it lends itself to demagogues gaining power through oratory six feet above comprehension, and it's certainly not communication.

4 One of the characteristics of the best examples of communication, such as Alistair Cook's *Letter from America*, is their

use of verbal illustrations to make their point. I remember Bertram Mycock, another fine and well-known radio broadcaster in his day, talk of the need for 'f'rinstances' to drive a point home. But how rarely do such illustrations appear? Far too often one wades through, or is subjected to, a stodgy and indigestible diet of half-baked ideas, cold and ungarnished facts, and a bland stew of observations, lacking piquancy or flavour.

Contrast that cook's recipe for non-communication with Cook's own description of his craft as 'creating a modest sort of literature for the blind'. It is lively and relevant illustrations which are the hooks on which ideas hang: no hooks, and the insights and thoughts fall, lying forgotten and discarded.

Mind you, it sometimes takes courage to use illustrations, and to risk the criticism of fellow experts. Sir John Cockcroft once described to an audience what the reaction inside a nuclear power station was like, comparing it to the spontaneous internal combustion inside a haystack. Of course it isn't *exactly* like that at all, but the comparison was sufficient to give an immediate impression—though it was the top man who was prepared to give it.

All these examples are common in our brave, new, communication-crazy world. But their effect is magnified because of the curious fact that the words we use are not neutral, but have a power of their own. This power comes from two characteristics of words:

One is the use of words appropriate to the effect the author wishes to create. In his book *Straight and Crooked Thinking*—a superb guide to lucidity and logic which all communicators should read, though sadly it is now out of print—Roger Thouless argues that when Keats wrote of 'the casement window' causing 'warm gules' to fall on 'Madeleine's fair breast', he knew the effect he was creating. 'A red beam through the fanlight on Sharon's white chest' does not have quite the same feel, and this aspect of the power of words has been known through the ages by wordsmiths of all kinds: demagogues and dictators, poets and politicians, prophets and preachers. But harnessing words to move or influence people for good is hardly possible with the brief and garbled interchanges allowed us in our brave new world of immediate and anaemic electronic chatter, or the tight-lipped weasel words of the executive, too harassed or uncaring to bother.

The other, more sinister, characteristic is the internal power words have. This is not a new concept: the Hebrews believed that words had a creative power of their own, and for Christians too 'The Word' is a synonym for God the Creator. Nearer our own time Dr Johnson said 'a language is a dialect with an army and a navy', and the amount of emotion released when a particular language, from Welsh to Serbo-Croat, comes under threat, bears this out. In more mischievous fashion, we can see the power of words in scandal-mongering, where false rumour starts to create that which it wrongly suggests. But what power will be created by the new language of, say, the Internet? So far little thought seems to have been given to controlling the vast and potentially anarchic powers contained in this modern-day Pandora's box, and we face already the alternative scenarios of such instruments being used to help with life-saving operations in the Third World, or to provide pornographic popcorn for couch potatoes in the West.

I suppose there's just time enough for this country, all countries, to try to control the powers unleashed by this communications explosion, and reduce the personal and social costs involved. However, I am not optimistic, partly because some of what is happening is potentially beneficial, and decision-makers are always loath to throw out the baby with the bath-water; but also because personal understanding and international agreement are only possible when people talk to each other, which they don't do, or only rarely, using language which is itself potentially disruptive—which is where we came in . . .

Still, we can, as always, start with ourselves, and I suggest five ways in which we can improve our own communication with others, at work and generally:

1   Think before speaking. This is the age of the soundbite, of
    the instant opinion and comment, with a resulting devaluation
    of the currency of communication. Too seldom do I find
    myself wondering whether the gem I am about to utter is
    really worth saying, and too often find myself a chattering
    stream, rather than a deep pool, reflective, quiet and drawing
    people to it for refreshment.

2   Be aware of what is happening in the revolution in global
    communication, but let it be your servant, not your master.
    The Internet may give you an intensely fascinating window—
    literally—on the world, but it has built-in traps: friends of
    mine were recently horrified to discover how easy it was for
    their teenage children to access pornographic material of the
    worst kind; while their mother, a keen cook, was, after
    expressing an interest in chips on a bulletin board, subjected
    to repeated requests for more esoteric recipes from a culinary
    fanatic in Hackensack in America.

3   Use illustrations to make what you say live in people's minds,
    and stay there. Think pictures, and think people, are two good
    maxims: people are always interested in other people, and
    remember what you say by association and identification. It
    is far more memorable to say 'Wembley Stadium full' than
    'about 75,000 people', or to describe something as 'the size
    of double-decker bus' than to give exact dimensions.

4   Use humour in what you say, but wisely and within your
    natural communication style. As countless schoolboy essays
    have argued, a sense of humour is a sense of perspective and
    proportion, and the capacity to laugh at ourselves is one of
    the better British characteristics.

5   Above all, *listen*. It may seem strange that the most effective
    tool in communication is listening, but it's true. Try active
    listening techniques like asking questions to clarify your
    understanding, rephrasing or repeating what the other person
    is telling you, and using body language (such as leaning
    forward, looking the person in the eye, smiling and nodding
    in agreement) to encourage rapport. There are so many people

with problems caused by work or illness or family life, and often just being prepared to listen to them, with warmth, patience and empathy, will take them a long way towards finding a way out.

Meanwhile I shall keep looking at cars on the M25—it will help pass the time away as I sit in my stationary wagon, and maybe there will be a decrease in the number of antennae, and an increase in the number of people in each car—actually talking to each other. If so, it will be frabjous indeed!

PART FOUR

MANAGING YOUR CAREER

CHAPTER 13

Taking the Controls
Self-development

'Can you play croquet?' shouted the Queen...

'Yes!' shouted Alice.

'Come on, then!' roared the Queen, and Alice joined the procession, wondering very much what would happen next...

'Get to your places!' shouted the Queen in a voice of thunder, and people began running about in all directions, tumbling up against each other; however, they got settled down in a minute or two, and the game began. Alice thought she had never seen such a curious croquet-ground in all her life; it was all ridges and furrows; the balls were live hedgehogs, the mallets live flamingoes, and the soldiers had to double themselves up and to stand upon their hands and feet, to make the arches.

The chief difficulty Alice found at first was in managing her flamingo: she succeeded in getting its body tucked away, comfortably enough, under her arm, with its legs hanging down, but generally, just as she had got its neck nicely straightened out, and was going to give the hedgehog a blow with its head, it *would* twist itself round and look up in her face, with such a puzzled expression that she could not help bursting out laughing: and when she had got its head down, and was going to begin again, it was very provoking to find that the hedgehog had unrolled itself, and was in the act of crawling away: besides all this, there was generally a ridge or furrow in the way wherever she wanted to send the hedgehog to, and, as the doubled-up soldiers were always getting up and walking off to other parts of the ground, Alice soon came to the conclusion that it was a very difficult game indeed.

*   *   *

Mr Squeers' view of education was succinctly put to Nicholas Nickleby: 'C-l-e-a-n, clean, verb active, to make bright, to scour. W-i-n, win, d-e-r, winder, a casement. When the boy knows this out of the book, he goes and does it.'

It's surprising how many things have been invented, or discovered, by accident, as someone has worked quietly on his or her own to solve a problem, usually not the one the newly-found product addresses. For example, penicillin was discovered in 1928 when Sir Alexander Fleming noticed during his research that mould growing on a bacterial culture was destroying the bacteria in its vicinity. Blotting paper was the result of ink accidentally falling on unsized paper while a keen employee was writing notes on the paper-making process. And 'Post-It' notes were a by-product of a 3M worker who, while working on his own to develop adhesives, found that the particular mix he had formulated had peculiar properties for an adhesive—strong enough to stick to surfaces, but weak enough to be peeled off to be used again. He took it to the Marketing Department, who didn't want to know, and eventually made them up into something like the pads we now know. He distributed them to senior managers in 3M, and, when they had (inevitably) become addicted to them, returned to sell the idea of developing them as a product. The rest is history, and a particularly successful history for the man who 'adhered' to promoting the use of his strange discovery.

Now it happens that 3M encourages its employees to experiment on their own, to 'moonlight' by developing their knowledge at the expense of, but much to the advantage of, the company. That is not usually the way it works in companies, with people competing for limited learning resources, the tools given being inappropriate for the task, nobody knowing the rules, or taking no notice if they do, and all in the context of senior management shouting for progress to be made and a result achieved. Exactly like the Queen of Hearts' croquet game . . .

When I taught at Sundridge Park Management Centre, we fought continually to set the training which managers received in a context helpful to both the individual and the company he or she came from, in other words as part of an overall process in the learning organisation. Sadly it was not always a battle we won, and all too often course members would admit that they were there because someone had said, 'Jack hasn't been on a course recently: where would you like to go, Jack? Sundridge Park sounds good—it's got two golf courses round it . . .' Jack would then be sent off, and perhaps would actually be willing to learn something and go back fired with enthusiasm. The response would be immense silence, as colleagues and subordinates kept their heads down and ears closed, in the hope, usually justified, that after a week or two everything would quieten down and Jack would get back to normal.

But the picture is changing. For example:

Responsibility for personal and career development rests primarily with the individual . . . However, the process of training and development is a partnership between the individual and his/her line manager, with support and encouragement from the boards of the various businesses and the human resources (HR) function. Each 'partner' must commit to the process and be accountable for it if it is to succeed.

A leading UK company has stated this as the first underlying principle in its approach to management training and development. As this and other principles are being worked out, the aim has been to ensure that the organisation has a continuing supply of managers who have the well-rounded commercial, technical and personal skills necessary for the business.

For that company, fair enough. But did you notice the phrases:

'Responsibility for personal and career development rests primarily with the individual' and 'each partner must commit . . . and be accountable for it if it is to succeed'? That's a revolutionary statement indeed, and one which employees have suspected for some time, but rarely seen stated so clearly. And although it is welcome that individuals can take more responsibility for their career development (and it is a recurrent theme throughout this book), such a statement is threatening too, raising many questions from individuals: How *do* I take responsibility for my development? Can I, and do I have to? How will I get fulfilment out of what I'm doing? What can I now do in this organisation? What plans do you have for me, and how do they fit in with these personal plans you say I must have?

The concerns are all the more serious because it is not just high-fliers any more who are the focus of attention. For example, how might a company manage its sales reps under the new approach? The simple answer is by empowering them to make decisions: the organisation establishes a mission and vision, then trusts people to carry them out. So the organisation has to build a framework for developing its people and encouraging self-development. But individuals have to take on that responsibility as well, and that's where the threat is felt.

A similar view has been taken by a European bank. A senior manager there has stated: 'The bank doesn't just encourage, but requires, people to take their development seriously. There is an investment the individual and the employer make to increase the return on the skill—both parties are beneficiaries.' The bank ran intensive technical training programmes, but individuals had to complete 26 hours of self-teaching to be able to be allowed to enter the programme. The bank's responsibility is to provide the facilities for individuals to access, and a trend is for these facilities to be those which can be accessed by individuals on their own.

As with any investment, however, there is a degree of risk and uncertainty for both employer and employee, especially when the employee is prepared to be innovative. Many of the initiatives taken by the bank in the use of secondments to Business in the Community or to overseas assignments originated with the employee. The risk element comes for the company when it is not clear how well the employee will act as an ambassador, and for the individual when it is not clear what happens at the end of the secondment.

Recently I attended a conference for student volunteers from a number of school sixth forms, who wanted to find out what it was like to be a manager. Several others and I helped them work through some team exercises, and provided an opportunity for each team to 'interview' us separately about life as a manager. I spoke to one student who said she was sorry her friends had not wanted to come, because she had discovered so much that was new, not least about herself.

In this management conference for students, there lies a fundamental illustration for all organisations: these students had taken time out with the agreement of their 'employers' (their schools, teachers, careers advisers, head teachers and parents) to find out something for themselves and about themselves. They were also getting the benefit of independent advice and resources about what it was like to be a manager. They could then use that information to calibrate their thoughts and future discussions with their 'employers', which would in turn contribute to their personal development plans.

I believe the future model for organisations, therefore, is one of a triangular partnership between the individual, the various representatives in an organisation and an independent third party (whose role may be to help assess development needs, or to provide the means of meeting those needs, or both). All three parties in the triangle have to fulfil their role to ensure the business skills needed are met and individuals are enabled to take responsibility for their development.

Organisations which recognise these responsibilities and build on this approach are going to win the commitment of current and future managers, because they will be turning themselves into what Charles Handy, in *The Age of Unreason*, calls 'the learning organisation'.

> Learning organisations [he says] want everyone to learn
> always, and bend over backwards to make that obvious
> . . . self-development contracts, recognised mentors, outside
> visits and seminars . . . are part of that. So are more formal
> arrangements such as tuition reimbursement schemes . . .
> more opportunities to listen in on higher-level debates in
> Japan, projects beyond the immediate job, the public encour-
> agement of questions at all levels, quality circles or their
> equivalent in study teams everywhere, brainstorming parties
> around new problems, horizontal careers to open up new
> possibilities, the encouragement of precocity and initiative
> even if it may offend, rewards tied to output not to status,
> to performance not to age, constant celebrations of achieve-
> ment and, above all else, a genuine feeling everywhere of
> 'unconditional positive regard' for the individual, or, in
> more sensible language, of *care* for the individual.

Becoming a learning organisation in this sense is not easy, but
needs to be worked at as a partnership—the kind of partnership
described above. It is, after all, the antithesis of those many
managers who were trained at the John Wayne school of management, and who are still alive and well and living in . . . well, I'm
sure you know some personally. These managers are adept at
building up and using the kind of obstacles to change described
by Rosabeth Moss Kanter in her book *The Change Masters*. She
studied a range of large American corporations and produced ten
rules for stifling initiative:

1 Regard any new idea from below with suspicion—because
   it is new and because it is from below.
2 Insist that people who need your approval to act first go
   through several other levels of management to get their sig-
   natures.
3 Ask departments or individuals to challenge and criticise
   each other's proposals.
4 Express your criticisms freely and withhold your praise.

(That keeps them on their toes.) Let them know they can be fired at any time.

5 Treat problems as a sign of failure.

6 Control everything carefully. Count anything that can be counted, frequently.

7 Make decisions to reorganise or change policies in secret and spring them on people unexpectedly (that also keeps people on their toes).

8 Make sure that any request for information is fully justified and that it isn't distributed too freely (you don't want data to fall into the wrong hands).

9 Assign to lower-level managers, in the name of delegation and participation, responsibility for figuring out how to cut back, lay off or move people around.

10 Above all, never forget that you, the higher-ups, already know everything important about this business.

So it may be true that in the best organisations individuals will in future have greater control of their career, but they can't do it alone, nor should they. They need the support and encouragement which only the organisation itself, and interested third parties, can bring.

Not that this is new . . . as long ago as 1830 Sir Walter Scott wrote in a letter to a friend: 'All men who have turned out worth anything have had the chief hand in their own education.' The surprise is that it has taken so long to filter through from Scotland to the rest of the world . . .

CHAPTER 14

Going for Goal
Focus on personal targets

There was a table set out under a tree in front of the house, and the March Hare and the Hatter were having tea at it: a Dormouse was sitting between them, fast asleep, and the other two were resting their elbows on it, and talking over its head . . .

'Have some wine,' the March Hare said in an encouraging tone.

Alice looked all round the table, but there was nothing on it but tea. 'I don't see any wine,' she remarked.

'There isn't any,' said the March Hare.

'Then it wasn't very civil of you to offer it,' said Alice angrily.

'It wasn't very civil of you to sit down without being invited,' said the March Hare.

'I didn't know it was *your* table,' said Alice; 'it's laid for a great many more than three' . . .

The Hatter opened his eyes very wide on hearing this; but all he *said* was, 'Why is a raven like a writing-desk?'

'Come, we shall have some fun now!' thought Alice. 'I'm glad they've begun asking riddles—I believe I can guess that,' she added aloud.

'Do you mean that you think you can find out the answer to it?' said the March Hare.

'Exactly so,' said Alice.

'Then you should say what you mean,' the March Hare went on.

'I do,' Alice hastily replied; 'at least—at least I mean what I say—that's the same thing, you know.'

'Not the same thing a bit!' said the Hatter. 'You might just as well say that ''I see what I eat'' is the same thing as ''I eat what I see''!'

'You might just as well say,' added the March Hare, 'that ''I like what I get'' is the same thing as ''I get what I like''!'

*   *   *

There is a story of two stone-cutters sitting amongst a pile of stones, chipping away at small blocks. They were asked what they were doing and one said, 'I am cutting stone' while the other replied, 'I am building a cathedral'. This sense of a goal and perspective on your work adds a totally new dynamic to the activities of purpose in what you are doing.

Some goals are very clear-cut, in fact, are almost imposed on you from the outside. Examples of these are instantly recognisable in the sporting world. Look at any athlete's expression of concentration and delight in winning an Olympic gold: they speak volumes about the hours, months and years of preparation, heartache and joy to be in peak condition at the right time. Rugby teams had training schedules set four years before the World Cup to get them to the point of winning. The goal was still there, even when it was defeated by the form of Jonah Lomu and a powerful All Blacks side.

These goals, whether short or long term, are nevertheless utterly discrete, and you either fall in line with them or not: there is no real choice and the end point is determined by the gold medal or a cup on a particular day's performance.

Business, of course, is not so definite and finite in time periods. There are many directions in which a company can go, and how is it possible to know whether you have arrived? A whole industry exists in the methodology of setting plans and objectives: nothing wrong in that, since this is how you stay in business and keep everyone focused. But is it sufficient just to stay in business? Perhaps a more significant question is to ask what an organisation

is in business for, since the answer to that sets the parameters
for other business goals. As the Management Focus page of *The
Economist* said recently, 'Bosses are shifting their attention from
designing a singly corporate strategy to shaping general organisational purposes—so that others, lower down the pecking order,
can design micro-strategies for themselves.'[1]

If this is right for organisations, then it should be a serious
consideration for individuals at work as well. What do I get up
in the morning go to work *for*? Perfectly valid answers are to
pay the rent or the mortgage, buy food, provide for a family and
so on. On a higher level, though, is the overriding purpose which
makes all these activities meaningful day by day. Some people
say, 'I want to earn enough money so that I can retire at 60 (or
55, or earlier . . .)' Brian Redhead, the late Radio 4 presenter,
wrote a personal perspective column for SAGA's magazine
specialising in retirement issues. 'When I was 45,' he once wrote,
'I was forever talking about retirement. Only another 15 years,
I would say. But I never continued "and then I shall . . ."; I
wasn't thinking that far ahead, I was simply looking for an escape
without having the courage to do anything about it.' This sense
of purpose, this overriding goal which may never be reached, is
what gives each of us the rationale for everything we do.

Sometimes we get wrong our understanding of what a goal is.
An interesting example of an *objective* masquerading as a goal
was John Kennedy's desire to get a man on the moon in ten
years. It was accomplished in time, but there was no overriding
purpose undergirding it which would have enabled the mission
to go on. Had Kennedy said the purpose was for America to be
pre-eminent in space exploration, the achievement of the first
space walk would have led on to even greater things. As it was,
the astronauts involved all had some sort of traumatic anticlimax,
often leading to breakdown or clinical expression, and NASA
lost its role, having nowhere to go.

Not that goals have to be (literally) as global as that. Is my
purpose at work to help people develop themselves fully and get
the best out of every activity they undertake? If that is the case,

then it will influence those decisions that face me daily: shall I give this piece of work to John when I know he will take two days over it, or shall I do it myself in half a day and 'involve' him in the outcome? Or, when I am right in the middle of a report Sheila puts her head round the door—her face tells me that she needs my counsel urgently but I am sure I can pick up with her later. On the other hand, shall I ever be able to recapture that look and that moment, and address her need at a time when she will gain most benefit?

Managers need to establish their personal purpose and goals, and to assess the degree of fit between them and the corporate goals of the organisation for which they work. Martin Scott in his book on time management in *The Sunday Times* 'Business Skills' series, says, 'we cannot master time unless we know where we are going.'

So how do we set about setting those life goals which lead on to the objectives we try to attain in the different areas of our life? Let me suggest a few right-brain exercises which may help:

● Imagine an aunt leaves you £10 million, with the strict condition that you can spend *none* of it on yourself or your close family. What will you choose to do?

● Then, when you have done that, imagine that the solicitor says, 'Well done! As it happens, your aunt also left you a further £10 million to spend *only* on yourself and close family.' Again, how will you set about this task? What will you buy with the money?

These two exercises will help identify your *values*, since any life goal you have should sit comfortably with your ideas about which things are worthwhile and which worthless in the way you live, or want to live. After doing them, try three more exercises which start to focus more narrowly on your life goals:

● Ask yourself what you would do if today your employer told you to take two years off, with full pay, and with your job kept open for you. How would you spend that time? What extra resources would you need? How easily would you be able to attain them? What would the new activity, assuming there is one, give you which your present occupation doesn't?

- If you could be anyone else in history or in the present for a day, who would you choose to be, and why?
- Get a sheet of A3 paper and build up a collage of photographs, pictures, drawings, preferably in colour and cut out from magazines or newspapers, which represent how you view your life at present. Then do the same to show how you would like your life to be. What makes up the gap between the two collages?

The answers to these questions may start the process of establishing the deeper aspirations inside you with regard to your occupation and the person you would really like to be. I am assuming you will be honest—after all there's nobody to fool except you yourself—and that, as Alice says, you mean what you say. For in setting life goals there *is* a great difference between 'I like what I get' and 'I get what I like'. Most of us, I suppose, spend our lives trying to attain the former, putting up with the character, the abilities, the opportunities we get, rather than being proactive and setting our own goals, and going all out for them.

- Finally, based on what you know or have found out from these exercises, draw a picture displaying the things you want to achieve in the future, if possible with an estimated time-frame. It could be a road or a river, winding through town or countryside, with objects, buildings, signposts indicating your goals; it could be a patchwork quilt, its panels giving pictures of those overriding goals you are set on achieving. Whatever it is, keep it by you, and use it to give you a graphic reminder over the months and years ahead.

All these exercises use the imagination, and imagination is one of the most powerful self-motivating tools we possess: I have a friend who was planning to buy a new car and, having just received a legacy, wanted something a bit special. He drew up a list of possible cars, and for each car weighted a number of factors which he thought important. The clear overall winner was a Volvo ... so he went and bought a BMW. Excellent as the Volvo was, he just couldn't imagine himself driving one and getting the same thrill as with a BMW.

Almost certainly you will notice that your goals cover different areas of your life, usually your personal ambitions, your family, your career and your community. And as you look at each different set of goals you will realise their interdependency—your career goals, for example, may have to fit into your family goals, and may feature heavily in your community goals and the way they are shaped.

Having established the overriding life goal, or goals, setting objectives is the next step: remember that all objectives must be SMART—*s*pecific, *m*easurable, *a*ttainable, *r*ealistic and set in a *t*ime-frame. Put another way, ask yourself:

- What exactly do I want to achieve? Be as detailed as possible.
- How shall I know when I have achieved my objective?
- Have I the resources to achieve my objective? If not, can I acquire them in myself, or through accessing them outside?
- Are those objectives realistic, bearing in mind my background, the current economic climate, the state of the market and sheer common sense?
- What is my timetable for achieving my objectives? Are there legitimate short cuts I can take? (Typically this timetable is about five years—a curious period of time in setting future objectives, since it is not so far away as to be beyond specific planning, and not so near as to prevent flexibility as the attainment of your objectives proceeds. An acquaintance of mine, if he is asked to comment on a situation or statement when he has been half asleep or just doesn't have a clue, looks wise and says, 'Ah, I just wonder where it will all be in five years' time . . .' He assures me it always works.)

Finally, there are targets to set, shorter-term objectives which we need to plan to achieve *now*—or at least in two to three years' time. Again the imagination is there to be used—Chapter 25 below suggests how.

For those who say they have no time to think about these things, time is there if you want it. It is amazing how much time can be found and work accomplished in the 48 hours before you 'have to' go on holiday for two weeks, or in the 24 hours before you have to go to that conference in Barbados you have suddenly been asked to attend!

Using the imagination in goal and objective setting is rather like drinking a certain brand of vodka: before I did it, I found the exercise excruciatingly dull and arduous. Now that my right brain can come into play (the operative word), it is fun, practical and the only way I can take a holistic approach to my life. But I do need to check on my progress from time to time, to see how far I have come already. It is rather like the man whose ambition was to study jade: he found an expert who would teach him, and turned up on the day appointed. He was somewhat dismayed only to be given a piece of jade to hold for two hours, and was then asked to come back the following week. This was all that happened for the next two weeks. On the fourth week, he was sitting in the room as usual when a visitor asked him what he was doing. 'Well,' he replied, 'I'm wondering about that myself. All I do is to sit here and hold pieces of jade, and this week what he's given me isn't jade at all . . .'

CHAPTER 15

Past Tense, Future Perfect
Devising your career plan

[Alice] smiled and said, 'If your Majesty will only tell me the right way to begin, I'll do it as well as I can.'

'But I don't want it done at all!' groaned the poor Queen. 'I've been a-dressing myself for the last two hours.'

It would have been all the better, as it seemed to Alice, if only she had got someone else to dress her, she was so dreadfully untidy. 'Every single thing's crooked,' Alice thought to herself, 'and she's all over pins!—May I put your shawl a little more straight for you?' she added aloud . . . 'and, dear me, what a state your hair is in!'

'The hair-brush has got entangled in it!' the Queen said with a sigh. 'And I lost the comb yesterday.'

Alice carefully released the brush, and did her best to get the hair into order. 'Come, you look rather better now!' she said, after altering most of the pins. 'But really you should have a lady's-maid!'

'I'm sure I'll take you with pleasure!' the Queen said. 'Twopence a week, and jam every other day.'

Alice couldn't help laughing, as she said, 'I don't want you to hire *me*—and I don't care for jam.'

'It's very good jam,' said the Queen.

'Well, I don't want any *today*, at any rate.'

'You couldn't have it if you *did* want it,' the Queen said. 'The rule is, jam tomorrow and jam yesterday—but never jam today.'

'It *must* come sometimes to "jam today",' Alice objected.

'No it can't,' said the Queen. 'It's jam every *other day*: today isn't any *other* day, you know.'

'I don't understand you,' said Alice. 'It's dreadfully confusing!'

'That's the effect of living backwards,' the Queen said kindly: 'it always makes one a little giddy at first—'

'Living backwards!' Alice repeated in great astonishment. 'I never heard of such a thing!'

'—but there's one great advantage in it, that one's memory works both ways.'

'I'm sure *mine* only works one way,' Alice remarked. 'I can't remember things before they happen.'

'It's a poor sort of memory that only works backwards,' the Queen remarked.

'What sort of things do *you* remember best?' Alice ventured to ask.

'Oh, things that happened the week after next,' the Queen replied in a careless tone.

*   *   *

One of James Thurber's stories describes various women who featured in his early life: one believed that if a light were turned on without a bulb in the socket, electricity would seep lethally into the room. But it was the suggestion from the black housekeeper that they 'go up de garrick and become warbs' which really got him going. Thurber didn't know where the garrick was, but it sounded sinister, and he was absolutely determined not to become a warb for anyone.

The world of work is much like this story: there are a lot of people using a lot of gobbledegook to tell us what we should do, resulting in misunderstanding and resistance where, in fact, the answer may be quite clear and simple (interpreted, the housekeeper was suggesting a trip to the garret to pick up dead wasps).

In search of such clarity and simplicity, I approached four people, representing different sectors, both private and public, to answer the question: 'What advice would you give a manager to attain success in the next century?' Life at work today can be exciting, certainly, but it is often far from secure. A survey in *The Daily Telegraph* recently showed that 70 per cent of the workforce feel less secure now than two years ago, and 31 per cent are afraid to take time off when ill. So what price survival, let alone success?

Sir Paul Condon, the Metropolitan Police Commissioner, had perhaps the most striking thing to say: 'Stay fit, find a good balance between your professional and your private life; trust your colleagues and give them headroom to grow, as they will rarely let you down.' The last remark may raise a wry smile in those executives feeling prickly between the shoulder blades, but few would argue with the earlier words.

It was advice echoed by Peter Harvey, chief executive of Dorset County Council, who, like all those responsible for planning the future of local government, had had to turn dinosaurs into *Homo sapiens* in rather less time than the normal evolutionary process. 'The successful manager in the next century,' he said, 'will be trusting, allowing staff greater flexibility to respond to needs, and open, encouraging new ideas from staff.' Other necessary attributes, he believed, were flexibility to cope with change and challenge old ways of doing things; resourcefulness to find ways of doing more with less; and the ability to communicate.

Peter Stemp, personnel director for the Automobile Association, mentioned the survey published by the Institute for Employment Research at Warwick University, which forecast a big expansion in jobs for managers and administrators by the year 2001: 630,000 more would be needed by then, bringing the total number of jobs in that occupational group to 4.9 million, 18.5 per cent of the total labour force. Those employed in professional occupations would also increase by up to 60,000, to a total of 2.7 million.

The watchword for Peter Stemp in preparing for future success was 'employability': successful managers in the next century, he believed, would be flexible and broad-based, with a business qualification and experience in different companies, different functions and different countries. They would be self-aware through 360 degree feedback and the sensitive use of psychometric instruments, and their management style would be empowering and facilitating, relating to others in a way which would bring out the best in them—peers and bosses as well as subordinates. They would 'own' their future, taking responsibility for their own self-development, to ensure that their skills and knowledge did not become out of date. The best analogy for Stemp was 'cross-country orienteering', where you use your own resources, internal and external, to reach your chosen goal.

Business schools and executive development centres are well placed to identify and evaluate the keys to future success. John Chadwick, chief executive of Sundridge Park, said: 'Born in the early 1970s and formed in the 1980s, the influential managers in the next century will not carry the baggage of corporate loyalty. Technical excellence, in 1990s terms of MBA content, will be a given. Rapid response and mobility will be the hallmarks of the winners, who will build ad hoc teams and use, coach, mentor and drive them to fulfil self-generated targets.

'Managers will be aware of their value and be accomplished self-publicists. In exchange for contracted commitments, they will want job experience and training to enhance the vital CV. Where they work, how long and with whom will become a balanced negotiation with their employer who, having been born in the 1970s and formed in the 1980s, will understand completely.'

It's all very well to talk about 'owning your future' and 'fulfilling self-generated targets', but most of us want to know *how* to achieve those objectives. If, like the White Queen, we were able to remember the future, quite possibly we should have no problem, but as we can't there is a sneaking suspicion in most of us, I suspect, that, if there was ever jam yesterday, there is none today—and tomorrow's jam, like tomorrow itself, never comes.

For whether we are employed, unemployed or self-employed, we are all thinking about the future, either in the immediate or the long term. The wise will take that thinking further and turn it into some kind of plan of action. The very wise will know about Personal Development Plans (PDP) and start drawing up their own.

Tony Watts, the Director of the National Institute for Careers Education and Counselling, has said: 'Action planning has been introduced in the early years of school, in relation to educational (performance within particular subjects) and personal (hobbies and extracurricular activities) as well as vocational matters. It has been applied not only in terms of "macro" goals like career aims but also in relation to "micro" targets like completing homework on time.' Individual plans are a part of the National Record of Achievement scheme, launched as a national system in the UK in 1991.

At school level there appears to be a framework within which individuals are encouraged and allowed to think about a plan for their future. What framework exists for those between sixteen and sixty, or is it just a case of figuring it out for yourself, without help? Does creating a PDP fall into the bracket of managing, serving as a member of parliament, or becoming a parent, which Charles Handy describes as being three of the most important jobs in life but with no training available?[1]

One thing is for sure: it cannot be a Plagiarised Development Plan. When it comes to managing future careers many individuals and organisations want the quick fix. 'That seemed to work well in your organisation; please just send me the material you used and I'll implement it straight into my company.'

Copying a process that works well elsewhere is very risky without understanding, for example, differences in culture and the adaptation necessary. So here are three suggested dimensions for a PDP framework to be constructed:

First, there is the issue of *private plans and public disclosure.* New Year's resolutions, for example, almost always fail. We say them to ourselves and mean them at the time, perhaps even commit them to paper, but they don't last. One of the key reasons for failure seems to be that we think we are going to do something differently but we don't do anything about the *context* or *circumstances* in which we live. The result is that everything seems to conspire against us, and we carry on doing things and getting caught up in the immediate tasks—as we have always done.

Peter Herriot, in his book *New Deals*, refers to individuals 'contracting' with their organisations about their own development. However, these individuals nearly always add, 'I'm unlikely to start the contracting process myself—it's too much of a risk. But if I'm encouraged or invited to start it, and if I actually do so, then my feelings will follow suit.'

There may be colleagues within your organisation, or friends outside it, whom you trust and with whom you can share your plan. There is nothing like sharing something private in public to make sure you have an incentive to make it happen. It may also increase your knowledge of fresh ways of doing so.

There is also a message here for organisations to create an atmosphere which allows people to talk openly about their own development without fear of being shot down in flames or having it taken down in evidence for future use against them. For instance, are openings in the organisation really publicised? Are there clear policies and practices regarding access to whatever development opportunities and resources are available?

The second dimension for drawing up a Personal Development Plan concerns whether such plans should be more concerned with *general direction or with specific details*. For example, a computer manager in a telecommunications company told me that he and all his colleagues had PDPs. He worked in a matrix of project and staff management roles and, for him, the PDP was ineffective if it was too specific. He needed to be more general in his planning and have some overall direction, since there were invariably conflicts between the different interests of his team. He felt the need to be supported by an external mentor who gave his plan perspective. 'If I'm lost in London,' he said as an example, 'and want to get to Dover via the M2, I need a map or a flying eye to ensure I don't get stuck in a one-way street going towards the M1.'

For most people, however, there has to be a certain amount of detail in specifying ways in which individual personal development can occur—for example, in project management, through secondment, by involvement with outside professional bodies, through attendance at courses or seminars, or, increasingly, by individuals seeing a niche, an opportunity to develop, and making a proposal to their organisation as to how such a development opportunity will benefit both parties.

Third, and building on this last point, it is important to *bring future dreams into everyday practical reality*. I recall the director of a financial services company who had no plans for the future until he received a jolt to the system by being passed over for promotion. He had been up to his eyes in various projects, and had not given due time and attention to considering the future. He did not leave the organisation (nor did he want to), but at least he ended up with a Personal Development Plan which he intended, in part, to share with the company. It would, however, have remained a dream from *Mary Poppins* had he not assessed how his personal agenda might fit the corporate plan. Incidentally, an added bonus is that the development part of his appraisal discussions is now a shared responsibility with his manager . . .

We live in a world which grows exponentially and in ways which are unpredictable. When British Navy cooks are today advised to 'place your table candles in the fridge for two or three hours before use, or they could burn unevenly', we are clearly on a different planet, let alone a different plane, from that which Nelson knew.

That does not, though, excuse us from making sense of present trends and making our own preparations for success. And if in so short a space of time we can move from nuclear fission to corporate vision, from total war to total quality, from global conflict to global markets, the future millennium may be brighter, and more successful, than we think.

There is no recipe for guaranteed success, or jam, in the future, but these suggestions may help:

● **Responsibility.** Seize every opportunity to extend your know-ledge and skill base, and take seriously continual professional development and the creation of a Personal Development Plan. 'Knowledge is power'.

- **Plan** your future. Get your organisation to widen your experience, perhaps by seconding you overseas or to another part of the business, or by extending your functional responsibility. Try to monitor the added value you bring to your organisation through the work you do.

- **Feedback.** Ask for constructive appraisal, to develop your strengths and improve your weaknesses. View psychometric instruments as tools of the Age of Enlightenment, not of the Inquisition.

- **Develop** a facilitative management style: your natural management style may be to the right of Genghis Khan, but even he learned to use subtlety and wit. It is empowerment, not power, which now identifies the future winners.

It is all logical, all common sense, but we human beings are not always logical. Why else would we find funny the caption to a James Thurber cartoon: 'If I called the wrong number, why did you answer the 'phone?'

CHAPTER 16

Me Ltd

Giving an account of yourself

The Mouse looked at her rather inquisitively, and seemed to her to wink with one of its little eyes, but it said nothing.

'Perhaps it doesn't understand English,' thought Alice: 'I daresay it's a French mouse, come over with William the Conqueror.' (For, with all her knowledge of history, Alice had no very clear notion how long ago anything had happened.) So she began again: 'Où est ma chatte?' which was the first sentence in her French lesson-book. The Mouse gave a sudden leap out of the water, and seemed to quiver all over with fright. 'Oh, I beg your pardon!' cried Alice hastily, afraid that she had hurt the poor animal's feelings. 'I quite forgot you didn't like cats.'

'Not like cats!' cried the Mouse, in a shrill, passionate voice. 'Would *you* like cats if you were me?'

'Well, perhaps not,' said Alice in a soothing tone: 'don't be angry about it. And yet I wish I could show you our cat Dinah . . . oh, I beg your pardon!' cried Alice again, for this time the Mouse was bristling all over, and she felt certain it must really be offended. 'We won't talk about her any more if you'd rather not.'

'We, indeed!' cried the Mouse, who was trembling down to the end of his tail. 'As if *I* would talk on such a subject! Our family always *hated* cats: nasty, low, vulgar things! Don't let me hear the name again

... Let us get to the shore, and then I'll tell you my history' ... Alice led the way, and the whole party swam to the shore ...

'Ahem!' said the Mouse with an important air. 'Are you all ready? This is the driest thing I know. Silence all round, if you please! "William the Conqueror, whose cause was favoured by the Pope, was soon submitted to by the English, who wanted leaders, and had been of late much accustomed to usurpation and conquest. Edwin and Morcar, the earls of Mercia and Northumbria ... declared for him: and even Stigand, the patriotic archbishop of Canterbury, found it advisable—"'

'Found *what*?' said the Duck.

'Found *it*,' the Mouse replied rather crossly: 'of course you know what "it" means.'

'I know what "it" means well enough, when *I* find a thing,' said the Duck; 'it's generally a frog or a worm. The question is, what did the archbishop find?'

The Mouse did not notice this question ...

'You promised to tell me your history, you know,' said Alice, 'and why it is you hate—C and D,' she added in a whisper, half afraid that it would be offended again.

'Mine is a long and a sad tale!' said the Mouse, turning to Alice and sighing.

'It *is* a long tail, certainly,' said Alice, looking down with wonder at the Mouse's tail; 'but why do you call it sad?'

*   *   *

I like the words I came across the other day in an American journal: 'We're all in this alone.'

Out of the hundred largest US companies at the beginning of the 1900s, only 16 are still in existence. In the UK, *The Times'* first list of Britain's 300 biggest industrial companies was published in 1965: only 32 out of the hundred firms topping that first list could be still found in the top hundred by 1995. During the '80s, a total of 230 companies—46 per cent—disappeared from the 'Fortune 500'.

Obviously size does not guarantee continued success. And what happens to companies has been happening, is happening, to individuals.

In the past ten years a number of writers and speakers have put forward the view that we should look at ourselves as a company. William Bridges, in his book *Jobshift*, is the latest. He advises that we look at ourselves as though we are self-employed—'be in business for yourself while still drawing a paycheck'. In other words, think of yourself as Me Ltd, a company within a company—it's actually quite a different way of thinking about yourself.

Seeing ourselves in this light involves changing our perspective, and giving ourselves the opportunity to look with different eyes at who we are and what we are doing, and taking responsibility for this. Whether that is a major or minor shift depends on how much we believe we are in control of our life and destiny at work, and how much we think we—and our careers—are shaped by 'them'.

It is said of John Wayne, when he was congratulated on being given an Oscar, that he replied, laconically as ever: 'I just stand there and let people act round me'. That's an attitude not uncommon among employees—to stand there, and let the world be directed, literally, around us. In subtle and unsuspecting ways we can slip into the habit of accepting that 'they'—parents, relatives, teachers, university professors, youth-group leaders, bosses, even the Personnel Department—have control over us. We have, however, always had opportunities to make choices and to choose our own path. And one way of doing that is to run ourselves as a going concern—Me Ltd—and to decide what business we are in, and what we are in business for.

If we are to run ourselves as a business, we need to draw up a proper balance sheet. Let's look more closely at that, and at our profit and loss account.

First we have our *assets*—not just our health, our education, our money and property, and of course our human assets, those people who are our human resources and who help make our 'company' operate, but also our own skills, which we have built up to invest in our lives. These 'investments' or skills are either for the short or long term, and they may have been bought at a price (time at university or, literally, the price of course fees), or acquired for nothing as we learn and grow from experiences on the job. If you have not recently taken account of your skills, let me suggest a simple exercise: choose one or two events in your past, at work or outside it, which you regard as being of significance to you in your personal development. Then ask a friend to sit and listen while you tell him or her what happened, and to write down on a sheet of paper the skills you were showing during that event: at this stage only one-word descriptions are necessary—for example, communication, leadership, persistence, courage—but afterwards they should be unpacked to give greater detail. Put adverbs in to describe *how* the skill was exercised ('sensitively', 'firmly', 'helpfully'), and also include the context to 'earth' the event. A full description might therefore read: 'Sensitively intervened in a difficult group situation to help team members co-operate with each other.' Later still, it is usually possible to group these skills into clusters, leading to some ten or eleven groups of skills, each containing separate, but specific, examples of where and how a skill was used.

There are also *debtors*—although, very often, this item carries little value on *our* balance sheet because we have never moved out of our small sphere of operations. Doing things for, and providing help to, others can mean that they will help us in the future. We have to learn to give in order to get. Not that such transactions are as callous or self-interested as that rather bald statement might imply—but it is a *balance* sheet, and networking is built up from contacts with whom we can enjoy a mutually beneficial relationship. These 'debtors', therefore, arise mainly as we try to move across the organisation, outside our own departments, or across other organisations, and build up our network with others.

Many items rarely appear on a company balance sheet. One such item is *good will*, though it can be a very important item on our balance sheet. In a similar way, Me Ltd is often engaged in extracurricular activities which never come into the working day—running a girl guide or scout troop, developing a keen interest in history, organising a wine-tasting club, or pursuing any other interest with zest and vigour—but which build up our reputation for commitment, quality and social awareness. All of these have a value in our team-building and value-added business culture. So how do we satisfy *our* need for personal enjoyment and recognition, and how might we build a bridge between our work and social life so that some synergy (i.e. 2 + 2 = 5) results?

Companies often need to be able to convert assets into *cash*, and have a degree of liquidity. How far can *our* investments or skills become liquid and be transferred easily into other parts of the organisation, or into different jobs?

We also have *creditors*—those to whom we owe much of who and what we are. Some of these are long term and necessary in keeping us viable or solvent: friends, relations, family; but there are others where perhaps the debt we owe should be paid off or reduced to more manageable proportions. The Alice Principle which runs through this book states: 'To be employed is to be at risk; to be employable is to be secure'. If we are too dependent upon, and therefore psychologically in debt to, our employer to keep us in our employment, we are highly vulnerable; if we have transferable skills and can move elsewhere should the need arise, perhaps because of a change in the market, we are more secure. One part of our company vision, or mission, should be to see that our 'creditors' are paid off so that we can become self-reliant and free from debt.

It is interesting that our employers also represent a different kind of liability, because they are really *shareholders* in Me Ltd—providing the investment needed for training and development, which will reap dividends in the future for all concerned.

Work in progress is the value of our present stock in the work we do: is too much of it stored away and out of date, or is it current, highly valued and in great demand? It is, or should be, the function of appraisal interviews, whether formal or informal, to assess and evaluate our personal WIP.

The *profit and loss account* is also to do with the current activities in which Me Ltd is engaged, but on a day-to-day basis. Where are our efforts being put, as we use our skills and sell our services in return for a salary and benefits? Are we selling the same thing day after day, or do we have a very flexible range of offerings which our employer can choose to buy as the occasion arises? Are we making allowances for depreciation of our skills by sacrificing some of our time and expense in keeping up to date and developing team or project skills, communication techniques or awareness of other disciplines?

Hopefully, we are making some *added value or profit* which we can put into retained earnings for future use. Or are we just living on past capital, or experience, and actually diminishing in value?

The balance sheet provides a useful model for (literally) taking stock of ourselves, using the perspective of a managing director reviewing his company, and looking at our strengths and our weaknesses to see if they balance, to assess our overall profit. Many senior executives of my acquaintance do this on a regular basis: they understand balance sheets and profit and loss accounts, and probably share Lord Justice Harman's view that 'Accountants are the witch-doctors of the modern world and willing to turn their hands to any kind of magic.'[1] Not everyone has that knowledge or ability, but the *general* approach is what is needed and most of us can understand that. So take a piece of paper, draw a line down the middle and start putting your liabilities on one side, and your assets on the other, as defined above: you may be more sound, or wealthy, in career terms than you think.

Where do we look for an independent auditor to ensure that our self-assessment is fair and true? One growth 'industry' of our times is that of the career consultant, dealing with career management rather than outplacement, to whom managers can come for a regular check-up and audit of the progress, value and prospects of their career. Like a financial auditor, the consultant needs to be qualified and experienced; like a financial audit, a clean bill of health can give immense reassurance to the individual concerned, often encouraging him or her to start a new venture, or at least tackle the future with increased confidence.

Taking account of oneself is not a new practice: in the Bible,

Daniel tells Belshazzar, 'Thou art weighed in the balances and art found wanting.' Hamlet wonders of his father: 'And how his audit stands who knows save heaven?' What is new, perhaps, is doing it in a more systematic way, one based on modern accountancy principles.

So try it—but don't make it as dull as the Mouse did in *Alice's Adventures in Wonderland* when giving an account of the Norman Conquest; it's a fun exercise, or meant to be, leading not to a surfeit of boredom, but to profit in the boardroom of Me Ltd . . .

CHAPTER 17

Shattering the Glass Ceiling
The distaff staff perspective

Just then a Fawn came wandering by: it looked at Alice with its large, gentle eyes, but didn't seem at all frightened. 'Here then! Here then!' Alice said, as she held out her hand and tried to stroke it; but it only started back a little, and then stood looking at her again.

'What do you call yourself?' the Fawn said at last . . .

'I wish I knew!' thought poor Alice. She answered, rather sadly, 'Nothing, just now.'

'Think again,' it said: 'that won't do.'

Alice thought, but nothing came of it. 'Please, would you tell me what *you* call yourself?' she said timidly. 'I think that might help a little.'

'I'll tell you, if you'll come a little further on,' the Fawn said. 'I can't remember here.'

So they walked on together through the wood . . . till they came out into another open field, and here the Fawn gave a sudden bound into the air, and shook itself free from Alice's arms. 'I'm a Fawn!' it cried out in a voice of delight. 'And, dear me, you're a human child!' A sudden look of alarm came into its beautiful brown eyes, and in another moment it had darted away at full speed.

*   *   *

As early as 1713, Anne Finch, Lady Winchilsea, wrote in her poem, 'The Introduction':

> They tell us we mistake our sex and way;
> Good breeding, fashion, dancing, dressing, play,
> Are the accomplishments we should desire;
> To write, or read, or think, or to enquire
> Would cloud our beauty, and exhaust our time,
> And interrupt the conquests of our prime;
> While the dull manage of a servile house
> Is held by some our utmost art and use.

One hundred and sixty-three years later, Queen Victoria wrote in a letter to Theodore Martin: 'The Queen is most anxious to enlist every one who can speak or write to join in checking this mad, wicked folly of "Woman's Rights", with all its attendant horrors, on which her poor feeble sex is bent, forgetting every sense of womanly feeling and propriety.'

A striking feature of the world of work over the past fifty years has been the steady increase in the number of women in paid employment. This has taken two forms: more women are working, and women now make up a higher proportion of the total labour force. It has been estimated that by 2006, in the UK, women will constitute 46 per cent of the total labour force—and the picture will be the same in almost every other developed country. Combine this with the trends towards increasing service sector employment and the growth of part-time, temporary and other 'flexible' jobs, types of work in which women have traditionally predominated, and one could be tempted to ask: 'Is the Future Female?'

If it is, it will be at a cost:

A 'Workplace 2000' forum, hosted by Office Angels, a UK secretarial agency, described these key elements in the current workforce:

- Men and women typically work in different sectors of employment.
- Women tend to be concentrated at the bottom of job hierarchies.

- Most part-time jobs are done by women.
- Women's average gross weekly earnings are just over 72 per cent of the average male level.
- Having children negatively affects women's earning capacity.

And this is an age of equal opportunity legislation . . .

Popular attitudes, particularly towards women, change slowly, and with difficulty. In my commonplace book I noted the results of a newspaper competition to write the first, spoof paragraph of a best-selling novel. It was won by the following entries—and if the novels of today reflect the values of tomorrow, we still have a long way to go:

> The camel died quite suddenly on the second day, and Selena fretted sulkily and, buffing her already impeccable nails—not for the first time since the journey began—pondered snidely if this would dissolve into a vignette of minor inconveniences like all the other holidays spent with Basil.

> He was a Portuguese who had never fished and she was a Chinese who couldn't cook rice; he had enough hair on his chest to make a coat for a very small Hungarian and the way she kissed it made him wonder why.

> Plgnthgr had hidden his mtskrthkl in the mothclenth, and now he had taken the beautiful and magical Mekthkn and her infant Trmyljp there, too, and they all trembled as they heard the fearful chthlems of the invading Hrnewrs just above.

For women wanting to enter management, the situation reflects the dichotomy outlined above—some progress, but slow and at a cost:

- Although there has been a marked increase in managerial and professional jobs—and the trend continues to grow each year—a speaker at the 'Workplace 2000' forum said: 'For a woman who looks at a management role, one of the reasons why you baulk at it, as well as fear of success, is that you think in order to achieve that I am going to have to become a man.'

- Many of the jobs that have disappeared, in manufacturing, coal-mining, ship-building and the like, were male occupations, and the positions created in the service sector are seen as 'female jobs'. There has also been a growth in the number of part-time, temporary and contract jobs, often needing keyboard skills. All this suggests that women may be better placed than men to meet the challenges of the labour market in the next century.

- The overall changes to patterns of work, breaking down the old model in which the only route to the top was through a continuous, unbroken work pattern and long hours put in at the office, should benefit women who, if they have had children, have always found the traditional pattern hard to match. In contrast, women have always possessed skills of adaptability, flexibility and capacity for change, which should be at a premium in the new labour market.

- On the other hand, emerging work patterns may be stressful for both women and men, and social pressure to reserve more jobs for men, combined with a lack of confidence amongst women, could halt or even reverse the present trend towards a growth in female employment.

- Moreover, even for those women who make it into managerial positions, the glass ceiling is still there, still making the top positions in organisations frustratingly out of reach.

THE GLASS CEILING

It is worth spending some time in exploring this concept, which first saw the light of day in the *Wall Street Journal* in the early '80s.

Valerie Hammond, Chief Executive of Roffey Park Management Centre, is an international expert in this area and, according to her, glass ceilings are still very common in UK organisations. In some ways, she believes, the glass has got even thicker, since with flatter organisations there is less opportunity to go up rather than sideways. She thinks the phrase is appropriate in the sense that going through glass *hurts*, but to describe the process would prefer 'stuck in the ice', or 'trying to swim in new waters'.

There are five key points to bear in mind in any discussion about the glass ceiling:

1 The 'dominant male' attitude towards employment is deep-seated, arising from the centuries during which men were traditionally the breadwinners, but nurtured more recently by such things as National Service in the UK, and even by the educational system. Thus during the Falklands conflict the then Mrs Thatcher was always depicted as a man, wearing military dress—a caricature which I suspect she did not altogether dislike . . .

2 Even when women do break through the glass ceiling, *they often glaze it over again behind them*—sometimes to avoid being accused of favouring one group rather than another; sometimes, as they say, to 'maintain standards'; occasionally they do it for reasons of elitism, to retain their exclusivity. Interestingly, the women who react in this way after breaking through tend not to be CEOs, but heads of functions. The theory, therefore, that having more women in senior positions would have a 'trickle down' effect, because they would serve as role models for other women, appears to be flawed—because of the attitudes of some women themselves.

3 In other countries cultural differences produce different results in women's attempts to climb to the top: women have been more successful in Asian countries, for example, but are subject to other problems and pressures, such as rights in marriage. In the USA there are more members of minority groups at the top of organisations, but not throughout the whole country, and not in proportion to the size of the minority. In Scandinavian countries women have broken through,

but they are still regarded as low in the senior management pecking order, and something of a loose cannon in their organisations—sometimes brilliant, often instrumental in achieving success, always unpredictable.

4   This (male) attitude towards female senior managers arises partly from the fact that there *are* differences between the two sexes, with men having goal focus and women possessing multi-channel thinking and a 'softer' creative approach.

5   It is not enough for organisations who want to recruit women into their more senior ranks simply to recruit more bright women: unless the culture and structure are changed too, these bright women will either waste away at the more junior or middle levels, or, more probably, leave.

Whether or not there are many significant differences between men and women as regards management style is still open to debate: some enlarge on the differences mentioned above, and go on to associate women's style with being more consultative, and with wanting to build on relationships rather than just issuing instructions. Others point out that notions of a particular 'women's style of management' may serve as just another stereotype which undermines individuality and obscures individual competence.

More recent research has considered whether some organisational forms or structures are 'gendered', with implications for women's ability to operate in them successfully.

So what can be done to improve the situation for women in general, and those in particular who are ambitious to break through the barrier to the top, whether it is made of glass or ice? As regards organisations:

●   Support networking initiatives, such as the UK's 'Opportunity 2000' (a self-financing campaign set up by 'Business in the Community'), 'Fair Play' (a joint government and Equal Opportunities Commission partnership to encourage regional consortia of local people to tackle equality issues), and

'Equality Exchange' (the employers' forum of the Equal
Opportunities Commission).

- Emphasise the business case for encouraging the employment
  of women at all levels: quite apart from the fact that there is
  no ceiling to the limit of the award an industrial tribunal in the
  UK can force an employer who is found to have discriminated
  unlawfully to pay to an employee, there are sound economic
  reasons for ensuring that businesses attract and retain the best
  staff they can find. In the rapidly changing marketplace of
  the next century, successful businesses will need to build on
  the ideas and creativity of their staff: recruiting from a restricted pool of talent simply does not make sense—business or
  common.
- The role of education is central, and expanding girls' aspirations is crucial: as a participant said at the 'Workplace 2000'
  forum: 'It is absolutely amazing that girls are outperforming
  boys at school, so why don't they achieve more in the
  workplace?'
- Encourage women not to limit their expectations and impose
  a glass ceiling on *themselves*; networking and mentoring can
  help.
- Realise that differences between men and women at work,
  in that they may be looking for different things from it, are
  a benefit to an organisation, not a problem.
- Focus on individual competences, not on gender.
- Avoid stereotyping in advertising, in interviewing and in
  expectations of employees.

And as regards individual female employees, Valerie Hammond
has this advice, based on her personal experience:

- Stay true to yourself: don't try to be a surrogate male.
- Keep in touch with women at lower levels than yourself:
  don't isolate yourself.
- Prepare yourself for advancement: gain a reputation outside
  your organisation, but in an area which the organisation
  respects.

- Get publicity—make sure you are known.
- Don't get—or stay—in a rut: go for the mainstream.
- Stand up for your beliefs—don't compromise.
- Network with other women aspiring for the top.
- Above all, don't give up.

In 1990 Roseanne Arnold wrote, in *Roseanne*:

> The only options open for girls then were of course mother, secretary or teacher. At least that's what we all thought and were preparing ourselves for. Now, I must say how lucky we are, as women, to live in an age where 'Dental Hygienist' has been added to the list.

I wonder, if this book is revised early in the next century, whether this chapter will still be necessary, or whether its points will be taken for granted because, like the Fawn in the passage from 'Alice', women will have found, with delight, their true identity, and at last be darting away at full speed.

CHAPTER 18

Old Age Penchant

A certain future at a certain age

'You are sad,' the Knight said in an anxious tone: 'let me sing you a song to comfort you . . . The name of the song is called "*Haddocks' Eyes*".'

'Oh, that's the name of the song, is it?' Alice said, trying to feel interested.

'No, you don't understand,' the Knight said, looking a little vexed. 'That's what the name is *called*. The name really is "*The Aged Aged Man*".'

'Then I ought to have said "That's what the *song* is called"?' Alice corrected herself.

'No, you oughtn't: that's quite another thing! The *song* is called "*Ways and Means*": but that's only what it's *called*, you know!'

'Well, what *is* the song, then?' said Alice, who was by this time completely bewildered.

'I was coming to that,' the Knight said. 'The song is "*A-Sitting On a Gate*": and the tune's my own invention' . . .

> I'll tell thee everything I can;
>   There's little to relate.
> I saw an aged aged man,
>   A-sitting on a gate.
> 'Who are you, aged man?' I said.

'And how is it you live?'
And his answer trickled through my head
  Like water through a sieve.

He said 'I look for butterflies
  That sleep among the wheat:
I make them into mutton-pies,
  And sell them in the street.
I sell them unto men,' he said,
  'Who sail on stormy seas:
And that's the way I get my bread—
A trifle, if you please.'

         *   *   *

But I was thinking of a way
  To feed oneself on batter,
And so go on from day to day
  Getting a little fatter.
I shook him well from side to side,
  Until his face was blue:
'Come, tell me how you live,' I cried,
  'And what it is you do!'

He said 'I hunt for haddocks' eyes
  Among the heather bright,
And work them into waistcoat-buttons
  In the silent night . . .
And that's the way' (he gave a wink)
  'By which I get my wealth—
And very gladly will I drink
  Your Honour's noble health.'

I heard him then, for I had just
  Completed my design
To keep the Menai bridge from rust
  By boiling it in wine.
I thanked him much for telling me
  The way he got his wealth,
But chiefly for his wish that he
  Might drink my noble health.

And now, if e'er by chance I put
  My finger into glue,
Or madly squeeze a right-hand foot

        Into a left-hand shoe,
Or if I drop upon my toe
     A very heavy weight,
I weep, for it reminds me so
Of that old man I used to know—
Whose look was mild, whose speech was slow,
Whose hair was whiter than the snow,
Whose face was very like a crow,
With eyes, like cinders, all aglow,
Who seemed distracted with his woe,
Who rocked his body to and fro,
And muttered mumblingly and low,
As if his mouth were full of dough,
Who snorted like a buffalo—
That summer evening long ago
     A-sitting on a gate.'

*   *   *

When Mike, who looks like everyone's favourite uncle, was, at the age of 53, made an offer which, Mafia-like, he could not refuse, he took early retirement. 'I couldn't *not* take the offer,' he told me, 'otherwise I should have been working for nothing.' Besides, he said, he was a national authority in his field, so forget mousetraps—*everyone* would be beating a path to his door.

Six months later, a sadder, wiser man, he thought differently: 'I love my wife dearly,' he said, 'but if I have to go round Sainsbury's one more Monday morning . . .' When Carlos was captured, he thought (jokingly?) that there must now be an international opening for a fairly mild-mannered terrorist, and wondered where he could buy a slightly used Armalite.

Mike's experience was not unique. For those with a '5' in front of their age it is much more difficult to get another job. At least Mike was reasonably fixed financially, for the pressure—and thus the difficulty—for older applicants for jobs becomes compounded in situations where there is a necessity to bring in an adequate income.

THE DEMOGRAPHIC REVOLUTION

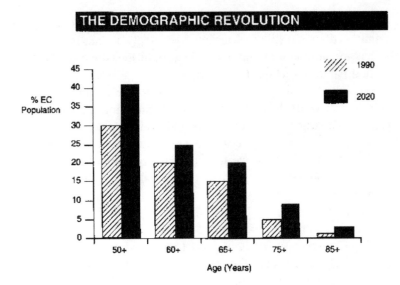

So what are the facts—as opposed to the myths—about getting a job in your 50s?

First, ageism can still be found alive in Britain—and, I suspect, in many other Western countries too. Although there are some shining examples of companies which give preference to older applicants—B&Q, for instance, has this written into its company policy—for most companies the big 'five zero' is the usual cut-off point as regards age, and even those companies which *are* prepared to employ older people often only consider them for the manual end of the managerial/clerical/manual scale. There can be a perfectly reasonable explanation for this: after all, Mike is a nice chap, but in a warehouse or retail environment, with page three pin-ups, cold tea and handleless mugs as essential components of the environment, he would be a fish out of water or, literally, an executive out of office.

It is a sad fact that more companies than should be the case regard older applicants as being much like the characters from the 'Looking-Glass' passage above: confused, like the White Knight's introduction to the song, with *outré* and outdated ways of earning a living ('I hunt for haddocks' eyes among the heather bright'—there's a killer of an interview reply!), and, above all, as having slow and mumbling speech, mild looks and a disconcerting habit of rocking to and fro.

Second, of the five ways of getting a job (there are only five)—working for yourself, using your network, targeting specific companies, replying to advertisements and registering with recruitment consultancies—the last two are virtually closed to older applicants, and the first, we find, only really works if setting up your own company has been in your mind and your blood for some time.

Third, some older applicants fail themselves by falling foul of the Scylla of complacency on the one hand ('Of course I'll get a job—everyone knows how good I am') and the Charybdis of being dilettante on the other ('I'm not looking for much—just the odd few hours per week to eke out the package and put some cream on the bread and jam').

So what advice to give to those over 50 who are re-entering the job market, or thinking of doing so?

1 **Acknowledge** that you do have considerable experience: you are not God's gift to industry, but you possess skills which may either be currently marketable or which can be developed with some retraining, and especially qualities which make older applicants for jobs particularly attractive to employers. I am thinking here of personal attributes like patience, wisdom, tact, understanding, perspective and commitment. Older employees tend not to be late for work, absent from work through sickness, or unduly ambitious: when I taught at a management centre in the '80s, one of the things we taught up-and-coming managers was to find and develop their successor; no self-respecting manager would dream of doing that now, since their identified successor might do just that, with disastrous results for the incumbent . . .

2 **Recognise** that employers may now be very open to the idea of a short-term contract—six months or one or two years, for

example. They are concerned about taking on fixed overheads again, but may be more than willing to consider a creative approach to working under contract—which is a far more realistic option for older employees, perhaps unencumbered by a mortgage or the financial drain of bringing up a family. This means realising for yourself that to have a job does not mean you need to have to hold on to it for the rest of your working life. Project-based careers can be just as much the norm for the glowing Roman candle as for the fizzing rocket.

3   **Give** serious thought to consultancy work—either on your own or with an established company. Consultancy is one of the few areas where age and experience work *for* you rather than *against* you. If you have a marketable competence plus reasonable people skills, this is always worth considering.

4   **Buying** a franchise could be an acceptable alternative. The amount of money required varies widely, but buying a franchise from a reputable firm can combine your flair and commitment with their support and advice, enabling you to avoid many of the pitfalls of going it alone. There are magazines and books devoted to this subject, and national exhibitions to attend. Just remember the two most important rules: don't spend too much of your hard-earned savings unless you are absolutely sure of a reasonable return on that investment; and remind yourself that to succeed with a franchise you must be sure you have the necessary drive and resources—can you stand the pressure of having to balance getting business and doing it, and what will you do if you are sick or injured?

5   **Learn** and reskill. The world of work changes constantly and there is always demand for new skills, or old skills reinterpreted and rehoned. In one sense the whole theme of this book is that managers—indeed all employees today—need constantly to be alert to trends in the job market, and to make sure they don't get left behind. One reason why IBM entered the PC market so late was because it was believed, at the highest levels in the company, that the idea of individuals wanting their own computer was a nonsense ... IBM

recovered, with incredible success, after failing to read the
trends, but it is not an example to be followed.

6 **Never** take 'no' for an answer: if you go for an opportunity
you really want and for which you believe you are ideally
qualified, always question a rejection. Politely, of course, but
firmly—now is the time for those assertiveness skills you
acquired. Try asking for help in analysing where you went
wrong, 'so that next time I will do better'. It is a variation
of what life insurance salesmen friends of mine describe to
me as the 'Parthian shot' technique. The Parthians, you recall,
had the nasty and unfair practice of turning round in their
saddles and shooting backwards, so in this technique, after
you have received a decided no-no, you ask precisely where
you went wrong, because the product, you believe, is basically
excellent. The theory is that the person to whom you are
trying to sell will agree that the product *is* good, and may
end up selling it to himself. I am assured it does work, though
in going for opportunities for yourself *you* are the product.

7 **However,** one way of avoiding going back after a no-no and
rebuilding the situation in this way is to lay your cards on
the table from the outset: say something like 'I'm a young
52-year-old, with just the sort of experience, I believe,
for which you're looking . . .' The worst that can happen
is that you get a rejection, which you might have received
anyway.

8 **Finally,** never give up. Mike worked assiduously at securing
another occupation, and refused to get downhearted at the
number of rejections he received. Rather like the dyslexic
devil-worshippers who gave their souls to Santa, he refused
to let his mistake get him down. Of course he was sensible,
and used his support network of friends to lift him up when
he was down; he used another network to look for new opportunities; and he acted proactively by approaching people and
organisations where he believed he had something to contribute. He set up a well-equipped office at home, attended confer-
ences where he could develop his network, and did not specify

too closely the areas in which he would be prepared to work.

I heard recently from Mike: he had just finished his first assignment working for a small consultancy, and was delighted, both with his first pay cheque, and with the fact that Sainsbury's now had to do without his custom, at least on Monday mornings, and the victims of international terrorism could now sleep more securely.

For him at least, a pension for life has been replaced by a penchant for living.

PART FIVE

CHANGING YOUR CAREER

CHAPTER 19

Plunged Into Darkness
Coping with redundancy

'Come, my head's free at last!' said Alice in a tone of delight, which changed into alarm in another moment, when she found that her shoulders were nowhere to be found: all she could see, when she looked down, was an immense length of neck, which seemed to rise like a stalk out of a sea of green leaves that lay far below her . . .

As there seemed to be no chance of getting her hands up to her head, she tried to get her head down to them, and was delighted to find that her neck would bend about easily in any direction, like a serpent. She had just succeeded in curving it down into a grace ful zigzag, and was going to dive in among the leaves, which she found to be nothing but the tops of the trees under which she had been wandering, when a sharp hiss made her draw back in a hurry: a large pigeon had flown into her face, and was beating her violently with its wings.

'Serpent!' screamed the Pigeon.

'I'm *not* a serpent!' said Alice indignantly. 'Let me alone!'

'Serpent, I say again!' repeated the Pigeon, but in a more subdued tone, and added with a kind of sob, 'I've tried every way, and nothing seems to suit them!'

'I haven't the least idea what you're talking about,' said Alice.

'I've tried the roots of trees, and I've tried banks, and I've tried hedges,' the Pigeon went on, without attending to her; 'but those serpents! There's no pleasing them!'

Alice was more and more puzzled, but she thought there was no use in saying anything more till the Pigeon had finished.

'As if it wasn't trouble enough hatching the eggs,' said the Pigeon, 'but I must be on the look-out for serpents night and day! Why, I haven't had a wink of sleep these three weeks!'

'I'm very sorry you've been annoyed,' said Alice, who was beginning to see its meaning.

'And just as I'd taken the highest tree in the wood,' continued the Pigeon, raising its voice to a shriek, 'and just as I was thinking I should be free of them at last, they must needs come wriggling down from the sky! Ugh, Serpent!'

'But I'm *not* a serpent, I tell you!' said Alice. 'I'm a—I'm a—'

'Well! *What* are you?' said the Pigeon. 'I can see you're trying to invent something!'

'I—I'm a little girl,' said Alice, rather doubtfully, as she remembered the number of changes she had gone through that day.

'A likely story indeed!' said the Pigeon in a tone of the deepest contempt. 'I've seen a good many little girls in my time, but never *one* with such a neck as that! No, no! You're a serpent, and there's no use denying it . . .'

*   *   *

Those who find themselves suddenly plunged into the darkness of redundancy know well the sad bitterness of the Pigeon's words, 'I've tried every way, and nothing seems to suit them!' They experience a range of emotions and reactions very similar to those faced in bereavement, with anger and a sense of betrayal high on the list.

Very often the individuals have been so committed to work and the tasks to be done for the organisation that they have given no time to themselves for planning what they should do in relation to their future. As one person wrote to me, 'Like all other employees, I now face the prospect of growing insecurity and the bare fact that middle-aged professionals are practically unemployable, because young men come cheaper.'

Now I didn't—and don't—happen to agree with this ultra-pessimistic view, but it is characteristic of those facing redundancy that for them the glass is permanently half-empty, never half-full.

The situation is made even worse by the fact that it is becoming more difficult to 'blame' redundancy on unavoidable factors. Back in the late '70s and early '80s, there used to be a stigma attached to redundancy, because, whether justifiably or not (mostly not), there was a feeling that it was being used to weed out the less competent, or the organisational misfits. Then, in the late '80s and early to mid-'90s, so many organisations shed so many staff that there was no longer any need to give an excuse for losing one's job through redundancy. As Eddie Obeng of Ashridge Management College says in his book *Making Re-engineering Happen*, 'In the past, if a person was made redundant, managers could usually explain the decision clinically and rationally. They could, more often than not, attribute blame to external factors such as depressed demand.'

Now, however, with new techniques like business process re-engineering emerging, there is less room to hide, less justification to offer. 'With re-engineering,' Obeng says, 'the argument is less easy for managers to put forward—they are saying that they are making changes for the future, or simply that the person's work does not add value to what the company does. Similar difficulties arise in explaining decisions to the people who remain.'

And as I'm sure every reader of this book knows from their own or friends' experience, the personal consequences of redundancy can be dire. The Pigeon illustrates several of them quite well—anxiety, energy and creativity in trying to find new ways to cope with the problem, growing disillusionment as none of the efforts seems to work, and eventually despair and a refusal to believe in *anything* any more.

People in this condition need very careful handling: some will be suffering psychological trauma, and may even be contemplating suicide, and for them some professional counselling and help should be sought as soon as possible. Others will be going through the up-and-down curve which characterises the common reaction

to shock: first a sharp downturn in emotions, as the news perco-
lates into the consciousness; then an upturn in the period of denial
('it *can't* be happening to me—I'm indispensable'); then another
downturn, as emotions like anger, bitterness, loss of confidence
and sometimes despair start to take over; and then a final upturn
in the period of acceptance, as recovery starts and determination,
self-esteem and hope begin to re-emerge. It is in this last period
that Mahatma Gandhi's words become relevant: 'Everything that
happens to you is your teacher. The secret is to learn to sit at
the feet of your own life and be taught by it.' But such learning
must be accompanied by action: Benjamin Franklin's comment
that 'He who lives upon hope will die fasting'[1] gives a practical
rider to Gandhi's teaching.

Assuming, therefore, that those who have been made redundant
want another job, or think they do, and are coming out of the
period of depression, back to a state where they are firing on
at least three cylinders, if not four (*and there is little point in
approaching the job market unless you are*), what should they
do? How should they proceed?

The first step is to realise that they are embarked on a marketing
campaign, and one of relative simplicity. After all, they have
only one product to sell—themselves—and only one sale to
make—you only need one job. Give that problem to most marketing people and they would reckon it a doddle . . .

Second, it is my experience, gained over a number of years,
that *a person who really wants a job will find one*—and that
view has been maintained and justified even through the worst
of the recession. Of course there are some factors that may effect
a person's success rate—age (if one is over 55 the range of
options does become much more restricted), time of year (the
periods around Christmas and the summer holidays tend to be
slow for getting a job) and willingness to be flexible over factors
like location, salary, type of contract and even the type of work
done—but determination to succeed *will* win through. Calvin
Coolidge, 30th President of the United States, said: 'Nothing in
the world can take the place of persistence. Talent will not;

nothing is more common than the unsuccessful man with talent. Education will not, the world is full of educated derelicts. Persistence and determination alone are omnipotent.'

Third, the campaign, or project, on which they are embarking is like all others, and needs:

- clear aims and objectives
- an action plan and timetable
- resources
- a budget
- progress reviews

It also needs a leader—the person setting out on the campaign.

So what sort of leader should you be? A good one, of course! But the stresses of being challenged to become a highly skilled job searcher affect people with varying degrees of severity, as we have seen, resulting in some faulty leader models:

All-action: Get there fast and first but in the wrong place, out of fuel and the team still waiting to be briefed.

Consensus: Exhaustive soundings before excellent response to today's problem—just in time for tomorrow's, different, problem.

Multi-talented: 'Learn' all the skills; 'listen' to all the advice— and then do it the way you first intended.

Procrastinator: 'Yes, that sounds right, but shouldn't we postpone until . . .'

Individualist: 'Team? . . . What team?'

Weary veteran: 'Yes, I've tried that . . . it didn't work . . . nobody gives me the right advice.'

You won't fall into those traps? Maybe not, but it's very easy to do, even for those who have exercised leadership skills at a high level. It is quite likely that job searchers will make some infuriating mistakes and suffer many disappointments as they conduct their campaign, so they need to marshal, and use, their resources. They can, of course, carry out their campaign by themselves—some do. But most campaign or project leaders recognise that they will be in a better position to set up and run a better project if they put all their resources available to full use. What are these resources?

- **The mind and body**—which should be looked after.
- **Close family and friends**—who want to help, and can provide immense support.
- **Colleagues and contacts** . . . and their contacts . . . and their contacts' contacts—if approached in the right way.
- **Professional resources**—which may be offered as part of a redundancy package.

If approached in the right way is a key phrase, because preparation is the key to job searching—and that is where the practical advice contained in the various chapters of this book applies.

And if you are in the unfortunate position of having recently been made redundant, consider these suggestions as the first part of your programme:

1 Make a list of fifty achievements in your life: they can be work-related, but put down others as well; they can be major ('coping with the onset of epilepsy'), or minor ('lopping off a difficult branch of a tree'); they can be recent ('being elected churchwarden at my local church'), or long ago ('becoming captain of cricket at my school'); short term ('completing a mini-marathon for charity'), or long term ('successfully bringing up my family'). Put them down, perhaps after discussing them with your partner, and look at the list from time to time, and always before going in for a job interview—it will boost your confidence, and give you a better perspective on the fact that you are coping with redundancy, which is but part of an otherwise rich and successful life.

2 Make up a collage of magazine pictures to express the best features about you; use colour, not black and white, to illus-

trate the various parts of you which are fun, helpful and successful.

3   Then draw the previous two activities together by writing a Capsule Statement, which is one or at the most two sentences describing how you see your role at work. Everybody, from job interviewers to people you meet a cocktail parties, asks the question 'What do you do?' So how are you going to answer in such a way that your thumb-nail sketch has impact, and is memorable to those you talk to?

4   Next write down a list of your key strengths, what you are good at, so that you are never lost for an answer if put on the spot. Be prepared to give actual examples to support your strengths, and group your strengths under technical skills, personal qualities (e.g. persistence, creativity, commitment) and man-management skills which have current market value (like team-building, motivation or communication).

None of the above will guarantee you another job quickly, but they will start the process of preparation, without which no job search can be successful. (The other ingredient is luck, which everybody needs, but which falls outside the scope of this book!)

Partners and families

A final word in this chapter, which started gloomily, but which I hope is beginning to show that there can be life after redundancy. Those closest to us when we suffer redundancy—wives, husbands, partners, children—often find themselves in a very pressurised, anxious state: they want to help, but often don't know how; they don't want to add to our problems by talking about theirs, but often feel the financial, emotional and social strain more keenly than we do. Sometimes a redundancy package includes professional help, and that's fine for us—but who helps those who love and support us? There is no easy answer, of course, but just being aware of the problem may help, and lead us to:

- Discuss the situation openly with the family.
- Share news of progress in our job search.
- Maintain some kind of normality by going out occasionally to the theatre, cinema or a restaurant, and most certainly by taking holidays, which are now more needed than ever.
- Appreciate that children, even young children, can understand more than we give them credit for, and welcome openness and the admittance that we are going through a bad time.

With careful preparation and use of resources, the job search following redundancy need not be disastrous, but may be the start of a new and exciting chapter in your life, and that of your family. The object is to regain, not just a job, but self-esteem and confidence, so that you can say, with that great old history debunker and motor manufacturer *extraordinaire*, Henry Ford: 'Whether you think you'll succeed or not, you're right.'

CHAPTER 20

The Search Goes On

Recruitment and selection

'Herald, read the accusation!' said the King.

On this the White Rabbit blew three blasts on the trumpet, and then unrolled the parchment scroll, and read as follows:

> 'The Queen of Hearts, she made some tarts,
>   All on a summer's day:
> The Knave of Hearts, he stole those tarts,
>   And took them quite away!'

'Consider your verdict,' the King said to the jury.

'Not yet, not yet!' the Rabbit hastily interrupted. 'There's a great deal to come before that!'

'Call the first witness,' said the King; and the White Rabbit blew three blasts on the trumpet, and called out, 'First witness!'

The first witness was the Hatter. He came in with a teacup in one hand and a piece of bread-and-butter in the other . . .

'Take off your hat,' the King said to the Hatter.

'It isn't mine,' said the Hatter.

'*Stolen!*' the King exclaimed, turning to the jury, who instantly made a memorandum of the fact.

'I keep them to sell,' the Hatter added as an explanation; 'I've none of my own. I'm a hatter.' . . .

'Give your evidence,' said the King; 'and don't be nervous, or I'll have you executed on the spot.'

This did not seem to encourage the witness at all . . .

'You may go,' said the King . . . 'Call the next witness! . . . What do you know about this business?' [he] said to Alice.

'Nothing,' said Alice.

'Nothing *whatever*?' persisted the King.

'Nothing whatever,' said Alice . . .

'There's more evidence to come yet, please your Majesty,' said the White Rabbit, jumping up in a great hurry; 'this paper has just been picked up . . . it's a set of verses.' . . .

'Read them,' said the King.

The White Rabbit put on his spectacles . . .

> 'They told me you had been to her,
> And mentioned me to him:
> She gave me a good character,
> But said I could not swim.'

.   .   .

'If any one of [the jury] can explain it,' said Alice . . . 'I'll give him sixpence. *I* don't believe there's an atom of meaning in it.' . . .

'If there's no meaning in it,' said the King, 'that saves a world of trouble, you know, as we needn't try to find any. And yet I don't know,' he went on, spreading out the verses on his knee, and looking at them with one eye; 'I seem to see some meaning in them, after all. "*—said I could not swim*—" you can't swim, can you?' he added, turning to the Knave.

The Knave shook his head sadly. 'Do I look like it?' he said. (Which he certainly did *not*, being made entirely of cardboard.)

'All right, so far,' said the King . . .

*   *   *

At the beginning of the seventeenth century, John Donne wrote in the elegy 'On His Mistress':

> By our first strange and fatal interview,
> By all desires which thereof did ensue.

Recently in this century, the American Fred Wolf wrote: 'The first time I walked into a trophy shop, I looked around and thought to myself, "This guy is *good*!" '

Anyone who has been for a job interview recently will, with a *little* artistic licence, immediately sympathise with the sentiments of both quotations—the feelings engendered by first interviews, often 'fatal', but often whetting the appetite for the particular job applied for, and the realisation that the greater the number of 'trophies' or achievements acquired, the easier the process of being successful may be.

Of the four ways of getting a job with an organisation (that is, not self-employment), recruitment agencies and advertisements are probably the most widely known, though not the most commonly used or the most successful: less than 30 per cent of jobs are filled this way, with targeting and networking, the subject of the next chapter, accounting for most of the rest.

There is, of course, an overlap between the two: recruitment agencies use advertisements as well as their own lists of candidates, companies may use both methods or just one to fill a vacancy. Both together are known as the 'visible' job market, inasmuch as the jobs they seek to fill are almost always genuine, known vacancies, open to anyone who may wish to apply. (The non-genuine ones are either positions in the public sector, where an organisation has to advertise by statute, but where there is already someone earmarked for the job; or vacancies falsely advertised in the media, not because they actually exist, but in order to send a message to competitors and customers about their supposed success. It is possible with the former that if you turned up for interview in a shiny light-blue suit with a yellow 'S' on a red background you might get the job, but there is no excuse for the latter . . .)

Advertisements are seductive for the hopeful job applicant because there (usually) *is* a job, and if it appears there is a match between what is wanted and what you are offering, it seems all too easy to send off the application and await the job offer, almost by return. Unfortunately, some six hundred other people will probably have had the same idea, so it is not quite as easy as it appears.

Replying to advertisements requires a certain frame of mind, and the observance of some simple guidelines:

1   The frame of mind should be one of enthusiastic effort, followed by realistic pessimism. In other words, put all you've got into the application, but then, when you have sent it off, tell yourself it is unlikely to be successful. That way you can only be pleasantly surprised if you do get called for an interview: you probably won't be. (This frame of mind, incidentally, is the logical justification for pessimism: you can only be 'surprised by joy', disaster and failure are expected . . .)

2   Be careful in assessing the degree of fit between what is really being asked for and what you can provide: it should be at least 90–95 per cent. A recruitment consultant of my acquaintance put it this way: 'Five years ago I could have put an advertisement in the papers asking for someone over 6' tall, able to speak Swahili, an expert skier with green eyes, and a qualified management accountant, and I might have expected three applicants with 60 per cent of what I was looking for. Now I'll get six people the next day with all, or all but one, of those requirements.' So check you have got the right fit.

3   If you are uncertain about the degree of fit, try telephoning the person handling the job application process, whether at the recruitment consultancy or the company, and ask whether the missing pieces in the jigsaw are vital or not. Sometimes the name of this person is given already, possibly with an invitation to telephone and discuss your suitability; if it is not, you can usually get the name by telephoning the recruitment consultancy or personnel department of the company concerned and asking who is handling the vacancy. Your reason for doing so is to avoid wasting time—yours and theirs—and it is often a good way of bypassing the system and getting yourself almost a guarantee of being on

the long shortlist. For that reason it is something to consider doing with all jobs for which you think you are particularly suited.

4   Send off the application, together with your curriculum vitae, both on white A4 paper. Some people wait a few days before doing this, reckoning that their application may get more attention if it arrives after the first rush: this sometimes works, but not if the person receiving the applications has decided to wait until a certain date before dealing with them all.

5   If you have to fill in an application form, bad luck! They are notoriously hard to complete, since they give you too much space for some things and not enough space for others, and you can't type on them, so your illegible handwriting will be exposed. The best thing to do is to fill in the first one you receive very fully, take a photocopy of it, and then use it as a template for subsequent forms.

6   Don't send a photograph unless you are specifically asked for one (they put people off rather than enhance your chances), but if you do have to, go to a professional photographer rather than emulate the man in the Hamlet cigars advertisement in one of those booths . . .

7   The letter you send should be simple, on one page, and consisting of three paragraphs: the first should contain the reference in the newspaper or magazine and the fact that you are very interested in the job (it is extraordinary how many people *don't* say they are interested, while companies do look for, and expect, enthusiasm. Saying 'of course I'm interested, why else would I apply?' is no excuse). The second should explain why you are the best person for the job, and cross-refer to the relevant parts of your CV or the application form. The third should express a hope of discussing your application further in an interview—which is all you want from your application: it's an interview, not the job, you want at this stage. Say something like, 'I should welcome the opportunity of an interview . . .'

8   There are many books written on CVs, so I won't go into

too much detail, except to say that a CV should not be more than two (occasionally three) pages long, with plenty of white space on each; you should list jobs in reverse chronological order, and emphasise achievements (what was different because you were in your previously job(s) and how the company benefited) rather than responsibilities (only used to give the dimensions of your job); you should use bullet points rather than continuous text for conciseness and brevity; it is perfectly all right for you to put your age at the end of the CV, but you must give it; and be careful with the 'interests' section at the end: companies like to see that you are well-rounded, but two examples I have had from applicants— breeding miniature poodles and collecting spiders—were counter-productive.

9   Finally, acquire an answering machine if you haven't got one: recruitment consultants or companies always want you yesterday.

Much of the above is relevant to dealing with recruitment consultants as well, except that the initial approach will come from you. Find out from books in the library who the main consultants are (*The Executive Grapevine* is among the best in the UK), and write a letter enclosing a CV, stating the reason why you are looking for another job, and wondering if they are handling any suitable assignments. Check by telephoning to find out whether there is a nominated consultant who deals with speculative approaches, and write to that person by name. If there isn't, write to the Managing Director or Chief Executive.

You are likely to receive one of 3.5 replies: the first response is a complete no-no ('We regret we have nothing suitable . . .'); the second is a little better ('We regret we have nothing suitable, but if we may, we should like to keep your details on our database . . .'); the third is best ('Will you please contact me or my secretary to arrange an interview at your earliest convenience'). The half reply is a curious one: sometimes you will get a letter saying, 'We have nothing suitable at present, but if

you would like to call in for a general chat, please let me
know . . .' Since these consultants are not lonely or short of someone to have tea with, always go, since it may well lead to an
opportunity. Often recruitment consultants are bidding for a contract, and want to have a suitable shortlist ready to produce if
they get it.

You may not get a reply from all those to whom you write,
but make a list of those who say they will keep your name on
their database, and remain in touch with them, perhaps by writing
or telephoning every six to eight weeks to enquire if any suitable
assignments have come up in the meantime. This way you will
not be a nuisance, but you will be letting the consultancy know
that you are still actively looking and not already in a job. It may
sometimes be possible to contrive to be in the vicinity of the
consultancy and offer to take the consultant out for a pub lunch:
putting a face to a name can help.

The aim of both the above processes is to get an interview,
the subject of Chapter 23, but the preparation for that interview
starts with your job applications, with setting out your stall in
the most attractive way possible. In the process of recruitment,
you may find many bad practices and many incompetent interviewers, exemplified in the Knave of Hearts' trial: trying to reach
a verdict before the trial; terrifying people with threats when they
are nervous; asking questions of the wrong people; trying to find
meaning and relevance when there are none—quite apart from
asking irrelevant or daft questions; and not least working on
false or ill-informed assumptions—as the American comedienne
Gracie Allen said, 'They laughed at Joan of Arc, but she went
right ahead and built it.'

At their best, though, recruitment consultants do get their man,
or woman. They have to adapt their approach, of course, to these
changing times, when a significant question is, 'Is it tough getting
business, or do the tough get business?' Most consultants, I have
found, will tell you that whether the job market is buoyant or
tough, it is always hard to get people of the right calibre.

Today, overall, there is a real shortage of people with a triple

A rating: *Acumen*—penetrating perception; *Ability*—fitness for the job; *Ambition*—looking forward healthily. Invariably there is an imbalance, with either too much ambition which, like Macbeth, 'o'er leaps itself', or so much acumen that there is little interpersonal skill.

To improve the search for the best candidates, there is emerging a curious practice by which companies employ search firms to find the right search firms to find the right search firm to do the search!—satirical echoes of Augustus de Morgan here, when 'great fleas have little fleas upon their backs to bite 'em, and little fleas have lesser fleas and so *ad infinitum*'. In the current climate, there are three key pressing concerns in the job marketplace:

1   While there is no such thing as a job for life guarantee any more, it is much more common to expect companies to be open to short-term appointments.
2   Now that there is greater fluidity in the market, companies are taking the advantage and replacing executives less suited for a growth phase. At the same time individuals at all levels are now thinking of moving because they have been in jobs for two years longer than intended.
3   Buyers say that different skill sets are now needed: not only middle managers but other key individuals have been laid off to such an extent that many companies now find themselves unable competently to service their markets; this has led to an increased level of customer complaints and a realisation that too often the baby has been thrown away with the bathwater. As a result the buy-back phenomenon is occurring, with organisations agreeing to pay anything in order to avoid losing good people and then having to struggle to find someone new.

All this circumstantial evidence adds up to some very important messages for both individuals and employing organisations.

At this time of change, therefore, there does appear to be a growing number of opportunities for people with the right skills

and experience—not least the skill of understanding the recruitment process itself. And that takes application, a willingness to
understand the pressures on those who do the recruiting, and
some persistence.

As someone once said: 'There are two kinds of people, the
successful ones who finish what they start and so on . . .'

CHAPTER 21

'Heard it on the Grapevine'
Networking

'. . . you can have no idea what a delightful thing a Lobster Quadrille is!'

'No, indeed,' said Alice. 'What sort of a dance is it?'

'Why,' said the Gryphon, 'you first form into a line along the sea-shore—'

'Two lines!' cried the Mock Turtle. 'Seals, turtles, and so on; then, when you've cleared the jelly-fish out of the way . . . you advance twice—'

'Each with a lobster as a partner!' cried the Gryphon.

'Of course,' the Mock Turtle said: 'advance twice, set to partners—'

'—change lobsters, and retire in the same order,' continued the Gryphon.

'Then, you know,' the Mock Turtle went on, 'you throw the—'

'The lobsters!' shouted the Gryphon, with a bound into the air.

'—as far out to sea as you can—'

'Swim after them!' screamed the Gryphon.

'Turn a somersault in the sea!' cried the Mock Turtle, capering wildly about.

'Change lobsters again!' yelled the Gryphon.

'Back to land again, and—that's all the first figure . . . Would you like to see a little of it?' said the Mock Turtle.

'Very much indeed,' said Alice . . .

So they began solemnly dancing round and round Alice, every now and then treading on her toes when they passed too close, and waving their forepaws to mark the time, while the Mock Turtle sang . . .

'Will you walk a little faster?' said a whiting to a snail.
'There's a porpoise close behind us, and he's treading on my tail.
See how eagerly the lobsters and the turtles all advance!
They are waiting on the shingle—will you come and join the dance?
  Will you, won't you, will you, won't you, will you join the dance?
  Will you, won't you, will you, won't you, won't you join the dance?'

*   *   *

Between 1982 and 1995, the number of mobile telephone users jumped from zero to over 4,000,000. Since 1985, homes and offices in the UK have added 1,700,000 fax machines. World-wide, e-mail addresses have grown to over 40,000,000. Close to 800,000 people in the UK now carry pagers, and an estimated 30,000,000 messages were left in voice mailboxes in the UK in 1994 alone.

As for the Internetwork, or Internet, this began with four host computers in 1969. Now it incorporates well over 15,000 sub-networks in over 70 countries, and these networks consist, in turn, of roughly two million host computers. Estimates suggest that by the turn of the century the number of Internet users will rise to anywhere between 80 million and 300 million, and that within a decade it will be as unusual for a person to be without an Internet e-mail address as it is now to be without a telephone number.

There are, quite clearly, a lot of people communicating with each other via just one form of network—the electronic one—and not all of them are ordering a midnight snack from Pizza Hut, calling the President of the United States, or learning how to dissect a frog (all possible now on the Internet). Network-ing is now an established part of life for millions of people, and the extent of it increases as the means or vehicles for it increase.

Not that networking is a new concept: Samuel Johnson's dictionary defines it as 'Anything reticulated or decussated at equal distances, with interstices between the intersections.' (Now you know: all suggested translations of this phrase to the Stanley Unwin School of English . . .) It is also what people have been doing for centuries when they wanted help, advice, or a favour, on a mutual advantage basis.

What makes it different today, and more important as a concept, is not merely its spread throughout the world, so that information and cross-fertilisation of a high order are available to people at an incredibly low cost: a weekday edition of *The Times* in the UK contains more information than the average person was likely to come across in a lifetime during the seventeenth century, and computer power is now 8,000 times less expensive than it was 30 years ago.

No, what marks out networking is the fact that it is a skill which can be applied by both those out of work and those in work—and unemployment and employment are alike the two main causes of pressure in our lives today. Many times I have heard individuals say that they wish they had treated suppliers, customers, colleagues and other contacts in a better way, especially now they have no job. They had been employed in one 'grouping' and are now having to 'regroup' into another job with another employer.

It is this second aspect of networking with which this chapter is mainly concerned.

Networking in this context is an informal approach to the hidden job market—a route to the jobs which have not been advertised and may not even exist yet. Someone, something or a situation has to put the thought into an employer's mind that he or she needs to 'buy' an employee. Networking is meeting people, both known and as yet unknown, talking to them, gaining information and new contacts.

Now, there are three myths about networking that we need to dispel:

First there is the 'I can't, or shouldn't, impose myself on other people' myth. Somehow it seems so threatening, even demeaning, to talk to someone else about needing another job. What you are doing in a networking meeting, however, is expressing your need for information which may help you. You may buy a new car straight from a garage having read a few magazines. You may have researched market alternatives. But, in addition, you will probably have met neighbours, friends, people at parties whom you have never met before, who will give you useful information about their own car. Then you make a decision. It is the same with jobs: people are nearly always willing to give information if asked in the right way, and very often other people will see your situation and skills in a totally different and helpful light.

The second myth is that 'networking will take up time and that's what I haven't got': that's a common ploy from those who are trying to resist doing something they regard as unpleasant or difficult. While it is true that it's quicker to respond to an advertisement, it is also true that at least five out of ten jobs never get advertised. Ask some people around you and you will be surprised how many obtained their present job through suggestions offered by others, or through chance remarks in conversation which they were able to follow up.

The third myth about networking is that you can only do it if you have learnt some arcane techniques, only available to the initiated, and that it is a strange and esoteric process not unlike the Lobster Quadrille. Certainly there is one element in networking which resembles a dance—which we'll come to later—but apart from that, it is a perfectly simple process which can prove to be immensely enjoyable. When I was made redundant, I could have gone on networking for years, so interesting were the people I met, but I had to get a job.

Networking, then, is highly effective in finding another job: as I said in Chapter 20, apart from working for yourself, there are only four ways of getting a job—responding to advertisements, registering with recruitment consultants, targeting employers you would like to work for and—networking. And the older you are, the more effective networking (and to a lesser extent targeting) will be.

But it is essential that you go about networking in the right way.

All too often people who lose their job, or who just want a move, panic and telephone all their contacts, all their friends and acquaintances, and ask if they have, or know of, a job for which they might be suitable. Almost invariably the people they ring cannot help, and then become strangely unavailable—always in meetings, and never returning calls—when the person looking for a job calls back.

The reason for this behaviour is quite understandable: people do not like to be embarrassed, and being asked for a job when you have none to suggest is deeply embarrassing, especially when you do actually want to help.

No, how you start the networking process is by drawing up a list of all those people you know who could be of help to you, bearing in mind that they should be senior enough to know of jobs at your level, and they must be *in work themselves*: retired people quickly lose contact with the world of work they have just left behind.

The next step is to ring up these people (some prefer to send a letter in advance, and then telephone—it's a matter of personal preference) and ask them for half an hour of their time for some *help and advice*. Everyone likes giving help and advice, and asking for this does not embarrass those you approach. It is here that you start echoing the whiting's words in the Lobster Quadrille: 'Will you, won't you, will you, won't you, won't you join the dance?' For of course those you approach know that what you want is not just advice, but a job; they also know that you know they know, and probably that you know they know you know. But they are not caused awkwardness by this knowledge, and so the door opens on the networking process.

When you do go to see these people for help, take your lead from them, and follow these simple tips:

- Don't take up more than the half-hour you asked for, unless they offer it.
- Take along a curriculum vitae, by all means, if you haven't sent one in advance, but don't get involved in a lengthy argument about it—the Latin phrase *quot homines, tot sententiae* ('there are as many opinions as there are people') is highly relevant to CVs: everyone knows how they should be done.
- Those you go to see will expect you to have some ideas yourself about future job possibilities: after all, when you go to the doctor and he asks you what the problem is, you don't say, 'I'm not sure—I thought you might give me some ideas . . .' So even if the ideas are not very well-defined, have an outline in your mind of what you would like your future career to look like.
- At the end of the time allotted ask for the names and telephone numbers of others to whom you can talk, using the name of the person you have been talking to as a means of introducing yourself.
- Above all, go in *listening*, not selling, mode: I have always found people helpful, and very perceptive in assessing strengths and weaknesses of which you may not be aware.
- If the person offers to send on to you some names and addresses, try to keep control of the process, and say that you will be moving around over the next few days, and promise to telephone the person's secretary for the details.
- Finally, write a note of thanks to the person you have seen when you get home (it's courteous, and provides hard copy for them to keep), and keep your network contacts informed about your progress. You may want to contact them again later, and they may continue as a very valuable resource in their own right when you get your next job.

Remember, anyone you meet may know of something which may help, or someone with whom you can be put in touch; at the very least they may talk about you to others behind the scenes, and these people in turn may become part of the network.

For those in work the same applies. The Personnel Standards Lead Body document—'A Perspective in Personnel'—says that 'senior managers are looking for processes which will bind the organisation together . . . so that the different parts of the enterprise pull together to meet customer needs and to share scarce or expensive resources'.[1]

The great guru behind Japan's industrial economic miracle, W. Edwards Deming, described one of his fourteen great principles for transformation as breaking down the barriers between departments.

During the 1980s the main target was to reduce demarcation, as companies tried to break down departmental boundaries, divisional walls or watertight compartments within organisations. The more successful companies have achieved remarkable successes in this, but the problem still remains in too many others—little empires within the organisation, and little cross-fertilisation.

Formal mechanisms may be used to bring teams together from different parts of the organisation, but teamwork is not just project teams and groups focused on particular activities in different areas of the enterprise. Teamwork is the whole organisation having a team mentality, and that derives from both formal structure, and informal networking opportunities. In this way individuals can find out for themselves not only what contribution they can make but also what resources are available to them in their endeavours. There is mutual interdependence.

Here is a practical way of helping yourself to operate more effectively by analysing and developing your own personal network at work—and in other areas of your life as well:

- First, get a sheet of A3 paper and draw a circle in the centre, with the word 'me' within it.
- List all the people you know who are connected with your work—bosses, colleagues, subordinates, suppliers, cus-

tomers, advisers or consultants—and put them around the central circle.

- Join the central circle to these names with a straight line: for advanced players draw longer lines to indicate the greater importance of the person listed.
- Write on one side of the line, in simple terms, what you believe you can do for that person, and on the other side what you believe that person can do for you.
- Look frequently at the list, prune those who cease to be important to your job, and add those who become important.
- Make sure you keep in contact with those on the list, even if no 'transaction' is involved.

Some people regard this process as cynical, but remember that one man's cynicism is another man's realism: what you are doing is codifying and organising one of your most powerful resources—people who are necessary to you in performing your duties effectively and well. I know that I should have been far more effective personally if I had used this technique when I was a Personnel Director, and the end result—a network to help you survive and succeed in your job—is known only to you. If you remove a person from your network you don't stop talking to him or her, but you may not make so much of an effort to go out of your way to make contact.

This technique can, of course, be applied to other areas of your life as well—social, family, community—again as a way of assessing priorities, and of allocating the personal and hard-pressed resources (time, energy, money and so on) at your disposal.

It is all a matter of perspective and of knowing the skills, attitudes and focus of people around you. When asked what it was like to win the Rugby World Cup in front of 60,000 of his own people, François Pienaar, the South African captain, said, 'There weren't 60,000 South Africans, there were 43 million South Africans!'

Looked at in that way, you can end up happily surfing the net, rather than snappily cursing it . . .

POSTSCRIPT ON TARGETING

I mentioned that networking is particularly suitable for older people wanting a new job. Another strategy is targeting.

The difference between the two is that with networking you are approaching people known to you, or known to someone who knows you and the person you want to see. With targeting you have no personal contact within the organisation, at least at the level or with the responsibility you require.

The process is simple, but there are rules:

1   Write to the most senior person relevant to the job you are looking for. This may be the Chief Executive, since although someone in that position will not be handling your application directly, he or she will pass it down to the person who will, and things have a habit of being dealt with faster and with more seriousness if they come down from on high (always check the correct name and title of the person to whom you are writing, by telephoning the company and asking the operator or the personnel department).

2   Research as much as you can about the company, so that you can suggest ways in which you may be able to offer added-value. It is no longer effective to say simply, 'I'd like to work for ABC Widgets'—there has to be a 'because . . .'

3   Such research can include the company's annual report, newspapers and newspaper cuttings libraries, reference books like *Kompass*, *Who Owns Whom* or *Key British Enterprises*, or electronic resources like Lotus One-Source of FT Profile or Freeway. Most larger libraries have these resources, or know how to access them. It's not that you need vast amounts of information, it's rather to show that you have done some homework and have thought about positive ways in which your skills and experience can benefit the organisation.

CHAPTER 22

Testing, Testing, Testing . . .

'Your hair wants cutting,' said the Hatter. He had been looking at Alice for some time with great curiosity, and this was his first speech.

'You shouldn't make personal remarks,' Alice said with some severity; 'it's very rude.' . . . here the conversation dropped, and the party sat silent for a minute . . .

The Hatter was the first to break the silence. 'What day of the month is it?' he said, turning to Alice: he had taken his watch out of his pocket, and was looking at it uneasily, shaking it every now and then, and holding it to his ear.

Alice considered a little, and then said 'The fourth.'

'Two days wrong!' sighed the Hatter. 'I told you butter wouldn't suit the works!' he added, looking angrily at the March Hare.

'It was the *best* butter,' the March Hare meekly replied . . .

Alice had been looking over his shoulder with some curiosity. 'What a funny watch!' she remarked. 'It tells the day of the month, and doesn't tell what o'clock it is!'

'Why should it?' muttered the Hatter. 'Does *your* watch tell you what year it is?'

'Of course not,' Alice replied very readily: 'but that's because it stays the same year for such a long time together.'

'Which is just the case with *mine*,' said the Hatter.
Alice felt dreadfully puzzled. The Hatter's remark seemed to have
no meaning in it, and yet it was certainly English.

*   *   *

She said, 'My name is Titania.' I had found her. I had been asked
by a new French managing director to find a graphologist to help
with staff selection, since he had used this method in his native
country. In the early 1980s it was not so easy to do this, but I
had eventually managed to track one down in the Essex marshes,
and now she was here, long-robed and looking like Madame
Arcati in *Blithe Spirit*.

Eventually she produced a report on each candidate, very
detailed, with a curious, spurious accuracy, like 'MOTIVATION:
58.6 per cent'.

There was no correlation between her recommendations and
subsequent performance.

Selecting staff, whether for employment or development or
promotion, is notoriously difficult, and the traditional way of
using one or more interviews is highly unreliable because they are
so subjective: 'Must be OK—plays golf off 7' (see the following
chapter).

A survey of different selection methods produced by Sundridge
Park Management Centre examined the correlation between
expectations at appointment and actual performance sub-
sequently. Interviews only managed 15 per cent, while phren-
ology (head bumps) and astrology came in at 2 per cent. No
selection method scored as high as 50 per cent, but assessment
centres, consisting of a number of different tests, exercises and
interviews, came nearest at 49 per cent.

It is this search for predictability which has led to the increasing
use of tests, particularly psychometric tests, in the job market
over the past fifteen years; applicants may now reasonably expect
some sort of test as part of any selection process—and should
welcome this.

The objective of tests is precisely that—objectivity. But do they work, and how should candidates for jobs approach them? We are, of course, used to 'personality' tests: which of us can easily resist checking in the tabloids how good a lover we are, or how ripe for stress-induced cardiac arrest?

Psychometric tests related to selection move us on to a different plane, but even here, where we assume statistical support in the form of reliability and validity checks, there are some odd-balls: 'Would you rather be a bishop or a general?' *may* elicit a piece of information crucial to determining my future, not least if I can't make up my mind whether I am more interested in plough-shares than swords, but I have my doubts. I believe its ambiguity, or lack of 'face' validity (i.e. does it look as if it will produce a credible result?), can actually be counter-productive: such questions can raise doubts about the authority of *all* tests, and clear a room full of intelligent job candidates quicker than Stevie Wonder with a flame-thrower.

Psychometric instruments have been around for a surprisingly long time, particularly in America—Myers-Briggs, one of the most widely used in the world, dates from the early part of this century. But it is only comparatively recently that they have been used in the UK.

As clinical and occupational psychologist Dr Paul Brown wrote to me about the use of Myers-Briggs in the UK:

> The day-to-day use of such rich information is still lagging behind. By contrast, at the Royal College of Defence Studies, participants from the USA armed forces have been familiar with Myers-Briggs for twenty-five years, know individual characteristics of their unit members and routinely use its data in coming to human factor decisions.

But the situation is changing: Robert McHenry, chairman of Oxford Psychologists Press, remarked in a letter to me that users of personality tests are becoming more sophisticated in how they evaluate and use tests. 'They want publishers like ourselves to take active stewardship over the tests, ensuring that research continues and that cultural and equal opportunities issues are monitored.'

Three issues seem to dominate discussions on such tests:

- First, there is concern about the ethical use of tests. There are codes of practice on the selection and administration of tests, and in the UK, training, licensing and test access are all tightly controlled.

  On the other hand, I was asked recently by a well-known company to 'fail' a candidate deliberately in a psychometric instrument, so that they could reject his application to go on a company-approved MBA course.

- Second, although we might have expected a trend towards the use of computers as an aid to the interpretation of tests, this is not the case. A lot of damage has already been done by suppliers who suggest you can use a computer to replace the human expert.

- Third, there has been a marked rise in extremely useful descriptive instruments—a variety of quick and colourful ways of describing teams, stress burn-out and selling skills. But the time is ripe for a whole new generation of instruments, which allow one to measure 'soft' data like management decision-making. The new data will be as much a part of forward decision-making as is a current cash-flow update.

As for types of tests, or instruments, there is an enormous number available. In the UK, everyone who wishes to be licensed to administer tests must undergo training for at least a week, with an exam at the end. Those who pass this can then be licensed under the aegis of the British Psychological Society, and can purchase tests from the various approved agencies. Among the most popular tests in the UK are:

- **The Myers-Briggs Type Indicator (MBTI)**, devised by a mother and daughter team in the USA in the early part of this century and based on Jung's type theory. It is now the most widely used instrument in the world, and looks at extro-

version and introversion as they affect a person's energy
levels in dealing with people; preferences in how data is
absorbed; the values/logical processes underlying decision-
making; and the way time is managed. It produces a four-
letter description (like ESTJ or INFP), which is clearly
understood by those who have been trained.

- **The Occupational Personality Questionnaire (OPQ)** and
the **Motivation Questionnaire (MQ)** are both produced by
Saville and Holdsworth in the UK: the former looks at personality under thirty factors, grouped into Relationships with
People; Thinking Style; and Feelings and Emotions. It is
widely popular and highly respected. The Motivation Questionnaire builds on current motivational theory, and identifies
those factors which motivate or demotivate a person at
work.

- **The 16PF (or Personality Factors)** is one of the oldest
instruments around. Lately available in a new version, it continues to appeal to those who are looking for a well-
researched, highly respected instrument giving an individual
profile with factors such as Warmth, Emotional Stability,
Sensitivity and Openness to Change. (I once asked a group
if they had ever heard of 16PF. 'No,' said one of their number,
'but I've heard of Edith Piaf . . .'

Others worth mentioning are the **Perception and Preference
Inventory (PAPI)**, owned and administered by PA Consulting,
and consisting of 20 personality factors, pictured as spokes on a
wheel, and the **Inventory of Management Competencies**,
another Saville and Holdsworth product, showing a person's rating in 16 areas of management against a normal population.
Unlike most tests, or instruments, this has to be computer marked.

I mention the above tests not because they are necessarily the
best, although they are all highly regarded, but because in my
experience they are the ones most people will come across at
interview.

The other highly popular instrument, now in the public domain, is **Belbin's Team Roles** instrument, which was thoroughly described in Chapter 7. Since almost everybody these days has to work in a team, the importance of 'Belbin' is greater than the original piece of research might have predicted. There is a computerised version of this instrument, and while I find the computer-generated reports better than most, I am generally suspicious of computer-based tests: I have seen too many people deeply upset by the strongly negative and damaging reports they have been given by a machine . . .

But whatever the type of test, the way you tackle them is all-important in doing yourself justice. The five points below are simple tips on your approach to the tests which could make all the difference to your results.

Remember that human beings are complex organisms; you are complex. And remember that the results are dependent on many immeasurable factors, including the skill of the person assessing the test. At best, the feedback interview after the test should be a joint enterprise, an overall perspective of the picture on your canvas, combined with an analysis of the layers of paint which make it up.

Perhaps the best attitude to adopt towards psychometric tests is a kind of credulous scepticism: at worst they can help to focus questions in interviews, at best they can reach parts of an individual which other means of assessment cannot. Certainly they don't have all the answers, they vary greatly in quality, not all of them allow for cultural and ethnic differences, and their effectiveness depends on the openness of the candidate and the sensitivity of the interpreter.

There is, however, a hidden, secret world in all of us, composed of hurts and hopes, past failures and potential successes, oughts and ought-nots, coulds and cannots; the best tests are able to unleash these, and help all parties realise the qualities which lead to a more fulfilled future. Rather like Madam Arcati, really . . .

TIPS ON TESTING—how to let your personality shine

- **Read**—carefully what you have to do. We are notoriously bad at filling in forms—I am still trying to pluck up courage to return to the mail-order company a device for removing hair from my nose, which I received instead of the alarm clock I thought I had ordered. You do need to ensure the information you provide is correct.

- **Speed**—work as quickly as you can. The first thing you think of is usually right: if you think too much about your answer, you will start getting into the spiral of 'what do I think he thinks I think I ought to put down . . . ?'

- **Truth**—don't try to 'massage' your answers. Yes, I know you want a job, but you want the right job, and don't want to be back on the job market again in three months. Most reputable tests have built into them questions which check for consistency in your answers, and which produce a rating for this factor. Many Personnel Directors I know will automatically reject an applicant if this rating indicates too high a level of massaging.

- **Feedback**—ask for it. Under the Code of Practice for administrating such tests you should be offered this, whether or not you are successful; but if you are not, ask for it. Sensitive, positive feedback can help you fill in more detail on the canvas that is you, and may even suggest different themes or scenarios to explore.

- **Challenge**—remember that psychometric instruments are only pieces of paper, and they are only as good as the people interpreting the results. Don't allow a simplistic observation at the feedback interview to go unchallenged if you really believe it is untrue. On the other hand, I have known candidates start with that reaction, and then add 'but wait a moment . . . if I'm honest with myself, that's probably truer of me than I thought . . .'

The Hatter is an appropriate character to illustrate approaches to testing: his is that of the consultant alluding to arcane mysteries, the person who borrows your watch to tell you the time. He speaks elliptically, with the kind of remark which 'seemed to have no sort of meaning in it, and yet it was certainly English.'

You will find people like that, of course, in the business of assessment, almost white-coated, and sharing Saki's view that 'a little inaccuracy sometimes saves tons of explanation'.[1]

But it doesn't have to be like that: assessment through the use of tests is now long-established and well respected, and the key to its mysteries reasonably available to all who wish to know. There may be a need to learn how to give sensitive feedback, though, for, as Alice herself says to the Hatter: 'You shouldn't make personal remarks'—or at least, perhaps, those which incite rather than give insight.

CHAPTER 23

'Come and Lie Down Here'
Interviews

She stretched herself up on tiptoe, and peeped over the edge of the mushroom, and her eyes immediately met those of a large blue caterpillar, that was sitting on the top with its arms folded, quietly smoking a long hookah, and taking not the slightest notice of her or of anything else.

The Caterpillar and Alice looked at each other for some time in silence: at last the Caterpillar took the hookah out of its mouth, and addressed her in a languid, sleepy voice.

'Who are *you*?' said the Caterpillar.

This was not an encouraging opening for a conversation. Alice replied, rather shyly, 'I—I hardly know, sir, just at present—at least I know who I *was* when I got up this morning, but I think I must have been changed several times since then.'

'What do you mean by that?' said the Caterpillar sternly. 'Explain yourself!'

'I can't explain *myself*, I'm afraid, sir,' said Alice, 'because I'm not myself, you see.'

'I don't see,' said the Caterpillar.

'I'm afraid I can't put it more clearly,' Alice replied very politely, 'for I can't understand it myself to begin with; and being so many different sizes in a day is very confusing.'

'It isn't,' said the Caterpillar . . . 'What size do you want to be?'

'Oh, I'm not particular as to size,' Alice hastily replied; 'only one doesn't like changing so often, you know.'

'I *don't* know,' said the Caterpillar.

Alice said nothing: she had never been so much contradicted in all her life before, and she felt that she was losing her temper.

'Are you content now?' said the Caterpillar.

*   *   *

There is a memorable sketch in the 1970s series, *Monty Python's Flying Circus*, which contains the words:

> Nobody expects the Spanish Inquisition! Our chief weapon is surprise—surprise and fear . . . fear and surprise . . . our two weapons are fear and surprise—and ruthless efficiency . . . our *three* weapons are fear and surprise and ruthless efficiency and an almost fanatical devotion to the Pope . . . our *four* . . . no . . . *Amongst* our weapons—amongst our weaponry—are such elements as fear, surprise . . . I'll come in again.[1]

Those who go for an interview for a job may be forgiven for feeling similarly confused, and there is usually some fear thrown in as well because of the inquisitorial nature of the meeting.

Interviews these days are enjoying a bad press; nobody likes them, they are known to give patchy results (in the survey discussed on p. 194, there was only a 15 per cent correlation between expected performance as a result of the interview and subsequent accomplishment—in other words, the interviewers only got it right once out of seven), and yet there is really no complete substitute for them—unless it be an assessment centre, of which interviews form a part.

There are at least three reasons why this should be so:

1   As has been pointed out earlier, there are few good interviewers around: it takes some skill to probe an interviewee so that he or she really reveals something about him- or

herself (barristers take years to perfect their expertise), and very few have it.

2 Interviewers are human, which means they sometimes do not concentrate properly, they don't listen, and they attribute unjustified qualities to those who possess other qualities held in high regard by the interviewer (the 'halo effect'). For instance, a golf-playing interviewer may overrate the capabilities of an applicant who plays off four. On the other hand, if the interviewer has had a row that morning with his red-haired partner, candidates with hair of a similar hue may be given an unsympathetic hearing.

3 There are some people who are verbally fluent, and who can talk their way into almost any job, regardless of experience or qualifications.

So be properly aware of the difficulties of interviews, remember most interviewers make their mind up about candidates within *ninety seconds* of meeting them, and plan carefully. This chapter is designed to help.

1 TYPES OF INTERVIEW

There are several variations on the interview theme: one to one, panel, assessment centres, and all with or without ability or psychometric tests in addition, and it is fair to find out in advance which type is going to be used and prepare accordingly.

One-to-one interviews

You may have a series of these, starting with a member of the personnel department and leading up to the decision-maker, who may or may not be the person with whom you will be working. First interviewers sometimes appear young—like policemen: don't be misled into thinking of them as inexperienced—they are likely to be very professional and alert.

Panel interviews

Relatively unusual in commerce and industry, but widely used in Government, Local Authority and Health Service organisations. The following points should be noted:

- all candidates are normally interviewed on the same day;
- the interview may be unstructured and therefore difficult to manage;
- it tends to be a formal occasion, usually with a Chairperson;
- a decision is normally made on the same day;
- panel members are often each responsible for one aspect of the application.

There is no magic solution to the problems of these interviews, but key points are:

- make eye contact with all members;
- give them equal attention;
- don't make assumptions about who is important;
- don't let being outnumbered cause you to rush your answers;
- don't panic if you feel you have not established rapport you are comfortable with—keep going.

Criteria based interviews

The purpose of this approach is to obtain and evaluate information on criteria or competencies critical for job success; it is based on the premise that past behaviour is the best predictor of future performance. The interviewer will try to pin you down in terms of what you *did*, rather more than an interviewer using the theoretical approach.

For example, a theoretical approach might be to ask you, 'What would you do if you had someone working for you who was confrontational?' The criteria based approach would ask, 'When was the last time you had to deal with an aggressive or unco-operative member of staff? What did you do?'

So think about past experiences which you may be able to use in the interview situation to illustrate behaviours you think will be relevant to the job you are going for. When you are asked a question in the interview, try to decide which skill is being assessed; take your time.

Examples of this might include:

'We all upset people at times. Tell me about an incident when you did . . . How did you try to correct it?' (SENSITIVITY)

'What specifically have you done to set an example to your staff?' (LEADERSHIP)

Even if you don't find the interviewer taking a criteria based approach, it is a good idea to prepare for one each time, as the specific examples identified will stand you in good stead during any sort of interview.

2 PREPARATION FOR INTERVIEWS

This is crucial, and needs to cover:

- How you will get to the interview—you may want to practise the journey.
- What impression you want to make through your appearance: suits are appropriate for both men and women, with darker colours preferable (men wearing lighter suits are regarded as being of junior to middle management level). Incidentally, it doesn't matter if you look at interview as if you have just walked out of Harrods' front window—interviewers always apply a discount factor, so if you look at interview how you normally look at work, he or she may think, 'What on earth is he going to look like when he turns up here?'
- Thorough research into the company, making use of all available business information, press comment, on-line databases and personal contacts.
- Which questions you are most likely to be asked, rather like the question spotting you used to do for exams. Use *Great Answers to Tough Questions* by Martin Yate to help you with the googlies you may get.

- Presentation statements, giving a capsule profile ('What I am'), career overview ('What I've done'), leaving story ('Why I'm here') and key strengths ('What you're buying in me').

3 QUESTIONS YOU MAY BE ASKED

Be prepared to give good answers to specific questions. Here are some:

About job attitude

- What do you look for in a job?
- What position do you expect to have in five years?
- Why do you want to work for this company?
- What are your long-term career objectives?

About your last position

- What did you like most/least about your last job?
- In your last position, what two problems did you identify that had previously been overlooked?
- Why did you leave your last position?

About you, personally

- Tell me about yourself.
- What do you look for in a job?
- What are your strengths and weaknesses?
- How would your colleagues describe you?

About your job approach

- What is your style of management?
- What do you feel are the criteria for getting ahead?
- What do you think 'communication' means?

About your accomplishments

● How creative are you?
● Give me an example of how you managed change in difficult circumstances.
● What are the most significant milestones in your career to date?

Miscellaneous questions

● What do you think of the business outlook over the next five years?
● What do you hope to get out of this job?
● What other jobs are you considering?

Questions YOU can ask

Choose these carefully, and show you have done some research by demonstrating a real understanding of the needs of the job. Two of my favourites are:

'Where do you see this department (or division, or company) in five years' time?'—which gives the interviewer a chance to hold forth on his or her opinions of the company. And . . .

'What kind of person succeeds in this company'—which gives you a chance of saying how you match the qualities which this question elicits.

4 ON THE DAY

● The golden rules are: be yourself; be on time; relax and enjoy the experience. NEVER LIE—you will always be found out!
● Take with you the details of the job, your job application letter, your CV and any relevant company or product literature.

- If you find it helpful, put in your pocket 3″ × 5″ cards for keyword prompts, and the questions you will ask.
- Get to Reception five to ten minutes before the interview time. Use waiting time to look at company literature or notice boards. Be careful of chairs in Reception areas: I have known candidates to get stuck in chrome and leather ones so tightly that they had to be helped out by their interviewer—not the best start . . .
- Remember that you are being assessed from the moment you enter the company premises—even in the car park (I once watched a candidate get out of his car in the car park, pick up his unshut brief-case, and shower papers all over the asphalt: he did not get the job . . .).
- Refresh yourself after the journey: leave coats and so on at Reception.
- Talk to receptionists or secretaries, but only if they have the time and inclination.
- Smile at the interviewer; give him or her a firm handshake.
- Listen actively, look interested.
- Answer questions briefly and positively: 'keep the ball in play'. BUT, if there is a period of silence, don't feel you have to fill it: that's the interviewer's job, but often an interviewer will refrain from speaking deliberately, in order to provoke the interviewee into saying something careless or unprepared.
- Remember the formula:
  'The situation was . . .'
  'The action I took was . . .'
  'The result was . . .'
  'The benefit to the company was . . .'
- Talk the employer's language. Remember KISS—Keep it simple, stupid!
- It's all right to ask for clarification, or to pause before speaking.
- Aim to get the interviewer thinking, 'I like this person: he/she would fit into the team.'

- The interviewer will normally indicate when the interview is at an end: establish what will happen next.
- Thank the interviewer for his or her time.

These are the basics: for advanced interview techniques study one of the many books on body language, such as Alan Pease's *Body Language*. Remember, however, that though this is useful in your understanding of what the interviewer is saying non-verbally, your capacity to use it on the interviewer is limited because body language is essentially subconscious. Degree-level interview techniques include the use of NLP (neuro-linguistic programming) to ascertain whether the interviewer speaks in visual ('I see the point'), aural ('That rings a bell with me'), or kinaesthetic ('I feel excited about the project') language, and then to use the same kind of words in return. This is like the physical 'mirroring', a body language technique to establish rapport by adapting your posture to copy that of the interviewer.

5 AFTERWARDS

Go over the interview: are there lessons to be learned?

Consider whether a follow-up or thank-you letter is advisable or appropriate—perhaps to underline a point or to add important information which you forgot to mention.

6 ASSESSMENT CENTRES

Used more and more frequently, Assessment Centres have several common characteristics:

- several assessors;
- several candidates;
- a variety of exercises;
- a participative approach;
- based on key criteria for the job.

The type of exercises used are:

- a line management interview;
- a personal interview;
- a group discussion;
- psychometric and/or aptitude tests;
- an in-tray exercise;
- a group problem-solving exercise, either a business simulation or a fun task like building the highest tower you can with Lego bricks;
- a presentation;
- occasionally, for very senior positions, a social gathering, to which partners may also be invited: also known as 'trial by sherry'.

Generally speaking, assessors will be testing managerial, personal and interpersonal skills once they are satisfied with your technical ability. In group sessions, the assessors will observe how you make decisions and solve problems in a team. It is important to use your initiative, but also to listen to the views of others, and assist the less able or articulate members of the team. In other words:

- play your part in keeping the discussion on track;
- encourage quieter members to make a contribution;
- avoid dominance;
- summarise;
- manage the time available;
- maintain an enthusiastic, involved and positive approach;
- think before speaking;
- practise active listening by watching others and building on their contributions.

You can't prepare for an Assessment Centre, but you can ask for feedback on how you performed. It will provide an insight into how others perceive your strengths and weaknesses, and demonstrates enthusiasm and interest.

So . . . inquisition or test of strength (and weakness)?

With the right approach, preparation and forethought, interviews can not only provide you with a reasonable opportunity to
shine, they might also be fun. As the catch-phrase went in the
popular television series, *The Fall and Rise of Reginald Perrin*:
'This one's going to be a real winner,' said C.J. 'I didn't get
where I am today without knowing a real winner when I see
one.'

PART SIX

PERSONAL GROWTH

CHAPTER 24

Machine Maintenance
Looking after your health

'You are old, Father William,' the young man said,
  'And your hair has become very white;
And yet you incessantly stand on your head—
  Do you think, at your age, it is right?'

'In my youth,' Father William replied to his son,
  'I feared it might injure the brain;
But, now that I'm perfectly sure I have none,
  Why, I do it again and again.'

'You are old,' said the youth, 'as I mentioned before,
  And have grown most uncommonly fat;
Yet you turned a back-somersault in at the door—
  Pray, what is the reason for that?'

'In my youth,' said the sage, as he shook his grey locks,
  'I kept all my limbs very supple
By the use of this ointment—one shilling the box—
  Allow me to sell you a couple?'

'You are old,' said the youth, 'and your jaws are too weak
  For anything tougher than suet;

Yet you finished the goose, with the bones and the beak —
    Pray how did you manage to do it?'

'In my youth,' said his father, 'I took to the law,
    And argued each case with my wife;
And the muscular strength, which it gave to my jaw,
    Has lasted the rest of my life.'

'You are old,' said the youth, 'one would hardly suppose
    That your eye was as steady as ever;
Yet you balanced an eel on the end of your nose —
    What made you so awfully clever?'

'I have answered three questions, and that is enough,'
    Said his father; 'don't give yourself airs!
Do you think I can listen all day to such stuff?
    Be off, or I'll kick you down stairs!'

*   *   *

Mahatma Gandhi was once asked what he thought of Western civilisation: 'I think it would be a good idea,' he replied.

I hear a lot from people about the expectations companies have nowadays of those who apply for jobs with them. Of course they need to be competent and be able to exercise judgement; certainly they need to possess good interpersonal and leadership skills and understand the importance of working in teams; necessarily they must be aware of how to succeed in today's fluid market and global economy.

But on top of these fairly basic requirements they feel pressurised to show, even prove, that they are fit, mentally and physically on top of life, intellectually stimulated and stimulating, in a stable relationship, and preferably with 2.4 children, who themselves are fit, mentally and physically, on top of life . . .

Now I understand how they must react to that experience: no one likes to apply for a job which he or she is perfectly able to perform, and then be made to feel two cocktail sausages short of a corporate buffet.

But companies have a point too: survival in today's world of work is tough, and in a very real sense only the fittest do survive. We may argue over what 'fittest' means in this context, but there is no doubt that physical stamina and mental keenness do contribute to vocational success. And that means the image of the corporate high-flier is changing: workaholics may satisfy their own internal drive but they are no longer seen to provide the creative, innovative, facilitative, sensitive leadership for which companies are looking: the argument is that if you are mentally mashed during the day you may become a couch potato in the evening, and that leads too quickly to a blunting of personal sharpness.

'But,' you say, 'that's all very well for you: I have so much more to do now that we've been downsized, there's no time or energy for finding time to boost my energy.'

It is not a new problem: the Victorians were putting *mens sana in corpore sano* on their blazers precisely so that young sprogs could achieve that balance in life which we seek today. The Father William verses at the start of this chapter are themselves a parody of a poem by Southey which has long been forgotten, while they have remained:

> *'In the days of my youth,' Father William replied,*
> *'I remembered that youth would fly fast;*
> *And abused not my health, and my vigour at first,*
> *That I never might need them at last.'*

And it is interesting that the Father William verses mention, as a recipe for mental and physical agility, the four ways in which people today approach the maintenance of their well-being: physical exercise, medications and treatments, diet and mental discipline. We may find them excessive, but who are we of this generation to criticise when some have their fat removed by liposuction, others, like Father William, do stand repeatedly on their head in yogic meditation, while others again try every kind of method, from drinking their own urine to applying live leeches to their skin, to retain some of the lustre of youth?

Life today is vastly more complex and pressurised than in

Victorian times, and whole industries now exist to cater for the
need, or demand, to be superman or wonderwoman at work, at
home, in the community, though I have yet to come across a
fashion for balancing eels on noses, or consuming whole birds,
bones, beaks and all—it is more often the bill that makes one's
appetite vanish. But anything is possible, so give it time, give it
time . . .

Faced with such impossible demands, it is not surprising that
some people take little more exercise than jumping to con-
clusions. And it is easy, of course, to go over the top: Stephen
Leacock, a Canadian humorist little read nowadays, wrote a short
story about a friend of his, a health freak, who used to take hot
baths to open his pores, and cold baths to shut them; he got so
that he could open and close his pores at will . . . The number
of joggers run down in the early morning gloom, permanently
unable to leg it through falling down roadworks, or savaged by
dogs resentful of these invaders working well beyond the plimsole
line, is legion. And I know many people who regard the need
for exercise, mental or physical, as just another reason for indulg-
ing in *haute couture* ('I managed to pick up this fabulous Gucci
sweatband, darling: only £99.95, and it has velcro made with
genuine barracuda teeth . . .') or for trying out the myriad pills
and potions, vitamins and vogues which call those in search of
perfection with their siren voices.

So I asked a doctor friend of mine what he thought the average
employee could *realistically* do to improve his or her physical
and mental quality. He gave me the seven vital suggestions listed
below, all of which are guaranteed to boost performance in the
workplace and promote a new sense of well-being; they won't
cripple you or your wallet, either.

1   **Watch your diet.** Talk to your doctor, visit a dietician if you
    can afford to, read one of the myriad books on the subject,
    but find what regime suits you personally (i.e. does it work,
    and can you stick to it), and follow it *quietly*—evangelists
    always did have a sticky time . . . If you need help to lose

weight, try doing so with a friend, or for charity, or with one of the many organisations which run groups to encourage you to stay with your objective.

2   **Find some form of exercise** that suits your figure and daily timetable: swimming and cycling are classics and suitable for all shapes and sizes, but not everyone can afford membership of a health club, even if they can find one nearby, and roaming dark streets or sharing public changing rooms with sweaty gymnasts or pubescent teenagers lacks appeal for many. Investing at home in a step, cross-country skiing or cycling machine, or something similar, may be an answer, particularly if it can be placed so that you can watch TV or listen to the radio or music while exercising (why does no one address the problem of the sheer *boredom* of taking regular exercise?). The decision must be yours—though do check with your doctor.

3   **Try to do simple things during the day which help:** climb stairs rather than take the lift; rediscover the pleasure of occasionally using two legs rather than four wheels . . . Take holidays in places where walking is a pleasure, and where you can't drive (like Sark in the Channel Isles) or daren't (like Madeira or Corfu). I like the story of Dr Johnson, the lexicographer and polymath, who was walking across hills with some fellow academics when he removed his coat, said 'It's a long time since I had a good roll', and proceeded to revolve towards the bottom of the slope at great speed.

4   **Read more, and more widely,** remembering the wise advice not to persevere with a book that bores you: go on until you find one you can really enjoy, and later the boring ones may be less so. One excellent way of introducing yourself gently to a wider range of literature is to buy, or borrow from the library, talking tapes: most of us like being read to, and it helps feed the brain as well as while away the time spent in jams on the motorway.

5   **Feed the imagination:** this will vary for each of us, of course, but might range from going more frequently to the theatre,

cinema or concert-hall, through exploring art galleries or museums, to reading Larson cartoons or doing the crossword. Try anything which for you will stimulate the creative, right side of your brain: the important thing is that it should be different, and challenging, and fun.

6   **Take up a new interest:** most of us have private, long-held wishes to do something really different, which 'pressure of work', or fear of failure, have prevented us from attempting. So challenge that assumption about pressure of work, and remember G.K. Chesterton's dictum that 'if a thing's worth doing, it's worth doing badly'.[1] I once went to an evening class entitled 'Painting for beginners', where the first task we had to attempt was to draw a cube, a pyramid and a sphere, in pencil, on an A3 sheet of paper. People around me were holding up their pencils as if in some strange, semi-pagan rite, but it did nothing for me. When my first three attempts looked like increasingly severe cases of piles I realised I wanted 'Painting for idiots' rather than the course I was attending, but it certainly made the problems at work seem quite minor by comparison and put them, literally, in perspective. So whether it's cooking, painting or sailing, it's the difference of the activity which refreshes the mind and sharpens our input at work.

   A word of warning, though, about computers: they are fascinating, and there is so much happening so fast that it is a bewildering bandwagon on which to jump. The degree of sophistication is quite staggering—it has been reckoned that if the same amount of progress had been made in the automotive industry as has occurred in the world of computers, a Toyota Lexus would cost about 7p, and would travel 600 miles on a pennyworth of petrol. But computers are addictive, and very anti-social, so use them carefully at home unless you want a quickie divorce.

7   **Don't take this aspect of yourself too seriously:** we are all the product of our environment, our background, our culture, and their influences are not always benign—sometimes they

result in eccentricities of self-belief. Alan Coren put it nicely when he wrote, in *Seems Like Old Times*:

I think I should feel considerably less rotten than I do this morning had I not learned all my anatomy from Arthur Mee's *Children's Encyclopaedia*. Never mind Ignatius Loyola, is my view: give a child to Arthur Mee until it is seven years old, and it will be his for ever.[2]

My doctor's advice is perhaps the start of an answer to Gandhi's words, and a modern equivalent of Father William's arcane activities: achieving, or reachieving, the civilising balance of a healthy mind in a healthy body. Eastern cultures have long sought this balance, and Eastern companies have incorporated national values into their own culture. Western cultures do not need to emulate Eastern practices—IBM employees used to sing company songs like:

> IBM, happy men, smiling all the way,
> Oh what fun it is to sell
> Our products night and day.

—but they may perhaps start with corporate institutions rediscovering their priorities. And that rediscovery in turn may result from individual employees achieving a balance between employment and physical and mental 're-creation' which gives true quality of working life.

CHAPTER 25

Let Me Take Me Away From All This
Taking holidays

'Oh, I've had such a curious dream!' said Alice, and she told her sister, as well as she could remember them, all these strange adventures of hers that you have just been reading about; and when she had finished, her sister kissed her, and said, 'It *was* a curious dream, dear, certainly: but now run in to your tea; it's getting late.' So Alice got up and ran off, thinking while she ran, as well she might, what a wonderful dream it had been.

———————

But her sister sat still just as she left her, leaning her head on her hand, watching the setting sun, and thinking of little Alice and all her wonderful Adventures, till she too began dreaming after a fashion, and this was her dream:

First, she dreamed of little Alice herself, and . . . as she listened, or seemed to listen, the whole place around her became alive with the strange creatures of her little sister's dream.

The long grass rustled at her feet as the White Rabbit hurried by— the frightened Mouse splashed his way through the neighbouring pool— she could hear the rattle of the teacups as the March Hare and his friends shared their never-ending meal, and the shrill voice of the Queen ordering off her unfortunate guests to execution—once more the pig-baby was sneezing on the Duchess's knee, while plates and dishes crashed around it—once more the shriek of the Gryphon, the squeaking of the Lizard's slate-pencil, and the choking of the suppressed guinea-pigs, filled the air, mixed up with the distant sobs of the miserable Mock Turtle.

So she sat on, with closed eyes, and half believed herself in Wonder-land, though she knew she had but to open them again, and all would change to dull reality—the grass would be only rustling in the wind, and the pool rippling to the waving of the reeds—the rattling teacups would change to the tinkling sheep-bells, and the Queen's shrill cries to the voice of the shepherd boy—and the sneeze of the baby, the shriek of the Gry-phon, and all the other queer noises, would change (she knew) to the con-fused clamour of the busy farm-yard—while the lowing of the cattle in the distance would take the place of the Mock Turtle's heavy sobs.

*   *   *

Queen Victoria wrote in her diary that when she sat next to Mr Gladstone at a banquet she came away thinking he was the clever-est man on earth; when she came away from dining with Mr Disraeli, she thought she was the cleverest woman on earth. Some people, some occasions, have the power to shift our self-perception positively, recreating our power to innovate and scintillate.

Holidays are meant to be one of these occasions.

But I have noticed so often, when I come back from one and look around the concourse at the airport, the irritable and exhaus-ted look on every face—and that's the group coming *back* from holiday. Where is the buzz, the sense of new purpose, the air of refreshed energy which presumably all of us hope a holiday will bring?

Now I accept that almost all forms of travel abroad leave much to be desired, and air travel more than most (I'm waiting for Torquemada Airlines to be launched—slogan: 'No Plane without Pain'). No one feels at their best when they have run their pesetas right down, find they have to wait five hours for a replacement aeroplane (courtesy of another airline, which already exists in all but name: 'Crocodile Airways sincerely regrets the delay . . .'), and then find their sterling or dollars have about as much acceptability for buying refreshments as Mauretanian bongo beads.

But can that really account for the lack of fun and positive benefit which seems to typify the holidays people take at any time of the year?

I would like to suggest five ways to improve our chances of having not just a holiday, but some recreation as well:

1 Do something different

We all presumably do something different from our work, but how about something different from our usual holiday? Our sixth year at Denia may have the advantage of familiarity and comfort, but does knowing that Benjamin's Bar sells the cheapest gin really outweigh the lethargy and the 'is this it?' feeling induced by repeating our experiences? I like the Costa Blanca, but take care to avoid it becoming the Costa Blanker. Two colleagues in the past year have been respectively on safari in the North African desert, sleeping under the stars and seeing the amazing rock paintings of figures resembling visitors from outer space; and white water rafting down the Grand Canyon, topped and tailed by two nights in Las Vegas: a mind-blowing contrast—from the vapid to the rapid, perhaps . . . Both trips provided mod. cons., with local guides, cooks and helpers, and both cost little more than conventional holidays, but my colleagues had, they said, the experience of a lifetime, and came back refreshed and invigorated.

2 Do something active

The holiday does not have to be physical, but at least it ought to be something which engages the brain. Doctors tell us that doing nothing, or very little, after retirement is the quickest way to an early death. Another way of putting it, perhaps, is that he who becomes a couch potato soon hands in his chips . . . From Open University summer schools to watercolour painting courses, from Murder Weekends to cookery classes, from gentle walks exploring the churches of Tuscany to learning gliding, the brain needs stimulation if that creative shift is to be achieved.

3   Do something creative

Now this is more difficult to achieve, since creativity, like happiness, cannot occur simply by trying for it: it's a by-product of other processes. There are, however, techniques which can help, and one particularly suitable for holidays is to devise or revise our *ideal scenario* for life. Take a sheet of paper, and write a paragraph on ten basic life areas (Job and Career; Money and Possessions; Friendships and Relationships; Home or Homes; Health; Travel; Leisure Pursuits; Self-Education; Creative Self-Expression—e.g. writing, painting, photography; and Contribution to the Community). Each paragraph should describe your ideal scenario as you see it now, and each scenario should be reasonably capable of being realised in three to five years' time, all other things being equal. And most especially, each paragraph must be written as if it has already happened. This is important, because writing in this way unlocks the imaginative or creative side of us, enabling us to *feel* what achieving this scenario would be like.

That's why I like the passage about Alice's sister in *Alice's Adventures in Wonderland*. For a short while she lets her imagination take her away from her ordinary surroundings, and shares the excitement, the adventures, the *difference*, created by Alice's recollection of her dream. Alice's sister knows—as do we all— that after that interlude, 'all would change to dull reality', but for the time being she is transported into a new world, and even when she comes back, she does so with 'eyes bright and eager'.

So your scenario might run: 'We have a time-share in Madeira, and also like walking holidays in the Lake District', or 'I am studying French at evening classes, and hope to qualify for an Open University course next year.'

The scenario can be written on your own, with a partner, or—perhaps most interestingly—you and your partner can write out your ideal scenarios independently, and then compare. Looking regularly at what we have written—say every month—shows us our life progress as a whole, and often leads to painting our scenario on a wider canvas, as we expand our picture of what we want life to be. It also gives balance to our perspective of ourselves, and of how we are progressing: if we are not doing well on one or two parts of the scenario, we may be doing even better on others.

4 Do something

In a sense, it doesn't matter what we do on holiday, provided that at some point we start refocusing on the most important areas of our life.

That should include spending some time thinking about our current job. Tom Peters says that all organisations should periodically be prepared to challenge, to call into question, their very purpose in existing, their goals, their *raison d'être*. There is surely a parallel here for individuals, and holidays—the right kind of holidays—can provide the ideal opportunity to rethink our work, our career, in a refreshed, creative way. Ask yourself questions like:

● Am I really fulfilled working where I am?
● If I'm not, is there a realistic alternative, taking into account my skills, qualifications, experience—and financial resources?
● If there isn't, is this a permanent state, or can I make up the gap by training, realising capital, relocating or just moving to another job, whether inside or outside my sector or industry?

5 Do something often

Remember that several short breaks are better for you than one or two long ones. In fact longer holidays can actually give you more stress, since the amount of preparation, particularly with children in the family, and the degree of trauma experienced in adapting to a foreign culture for what is at least 4 per cent of your year, can sometimes detract from the overall enjoyment of your hard-earned period of R & R. So try to get away more at weekends, or just for a day—the benefit can be out of all proportion to the length of time.

The Victorian era was one of the greatest this country has ever known. Was it by accident that as well as clever Gladstones there were also encouraging Disraelis to bring out creativity and innovation? If our holiday this year gave us some recreation, and a chance to consider our life plan as well as recharging our batteries, it would certainly promote our sense of well-being, it might promote our career—and arriving back at the airport might never be the same again.

POSTSCRIPT ABOUT CHRISTMAS

Of all the 'holiday' times during the year, Christmas is the most curious since it is a time when emotions run high, and the result is not always positive: maybe we miss someone who was close to us, or we look back with regret at some of the wrong paths we took, or we just remember with nostalgia the good times that were, but are no more.

It is for this reason that some people dislike Christmas—not because they want to emulate Scrooge, but because the pain outweighs the pleasure at this time. I hope that is not true for you, but if it is, I suggest three ways of combating the glooms:

● Try not to be alone: I know Christmas television can be good, but the twenty-third showing of *The Railway Children* is no substitute for real contact with real people, who hold you in affection and regard.

- Can you afford to get away to a different environment, to family, friends, a hotel or guest house, even one in another country? I once spent Christmas in Africa, and eating Christmas pudding in a climate of 80°F in the shade was more than enough to keep my Ghost of Christmas Past at bay . . .
- Above all, can you do something to help others in the community less fortunate than yourself? I have some friends, members of the Jewish faith, who every Christmas act as auxiliaries, willing to do anything, in their local hospice, thereby enabling some of the regular workers to spend time with their families. But whether you get involved in that, or Crisis at Christmas, or just visiting old and lonely people nearby, looking outwards as well as inside yourself can bring a new meaning to your Christmas.

At the risk of offending some, I could also suggest attending a church service, since although you may not have a faith yourself, such services, are, at the very least, marvellous aesthetic experiences, where beauty and dignity and harmony remind us of our humanity, and perhaps of something more . . .

CHAPTER 26

Mid-life Crisis?—What Crisis?

At this moment the Unicorn sauntered by them, with his hands in his pockets. 'I had the best of it this time!' he said to the King, just glancing at him as he passed.

'A little—a little,' the King replied, rather nervously. 'You shouldn't have run him through with your horn, you know.'

'It didn't hurt him,' the Unicorn said carelessly, and he was going on, when his eye happened to fall upon Alice: he turned round instantly, and stood for some time looking at her with an air of the deepest disgust.

'What—is—this?' he said at last.

'This is a child!' Haigha replied eagerly, coming in front of Alice to introduce her, and spreading out both his hands towards her in an Anglo-Saxon attitude. 'We only found it today. It's as large as life, and twice as natural!'

'I always thought they were fabulous monsters!' said the Unicorn. 'Is it alive?'

'It can talk,' said Haigha, solemnly . . .

The Lion had joined them while this was going on: he looked very tired and sleepy, and his eyes were half shut. 'What's this!' he said, blinking lazily at Alice, and speaking in a deep hollow tone that sounded like the tolling of a great bell.

'Ah, what *is* it, now?' the Unicorn cried eagerly. 'You'll never guess! *I* couldn't.'

The Lion looked at Alice wearily. 'Are you animal—or vegetable—or mineral?' he said, yawning at every other word.

'It's a fabulous monster!' the Unicorn cried out, before Alice could reply . . .

'What a fight we might have for the crown, *now*!' the Unicorn said, looking slyly up at the crown, which the poor King was nearly shaking off his head, he trembled so much.

'I should win easy,' said the Lion.

'I'm not so sure of that,' said the Unicorn.

'Why, I beat you all round the town, you chicken!' the Lion replied angrily.

*   *   *

I was recently reminded of this passage while sitting in my dentist's waiting-room. Leafing through the pages of a magazine, I came across some pictures of Sophia Loren—to me the most beautiful woman in the world (I realise, of course, the danger of making such a statement; when Paris made it of Aphrodite, the anger of Hera and Pallas Athene led to the sack of Troy. I shall probably get a sack of letters). She looked quite stunning, although I know for a fact that she is, well, over 60. I looked at the date of the magazine—perhaps it was from 1965, of similar vintage to the *Eagle* comic nearby?—but no, this was Ms Loren in 1996. How *does* she do it? One clue, perhaps, was given by the actress herself in the accompanying article: 'Ageing becomes a problem,' she said, 'only when you stop liking yourself. Fortunately, I still really like me, inside and out. But not in a vain way. I just feel good and comfortable in my skin.'

OK, I'll buy that—mostly. I know that people eat more healthily, look after themselves better, have more potions and unguents at their disposal than John Wellington Wells, and probably know more about themselves (and more deeply) than almost any previous generation; I know that because of all these things this is the way men and women can look these days, although few in my perception get near the ageless beauty of 'Santa Sophia'. I am even prepared to believe that 'you're as young as you feel',

and that being comfortable with yourself can be part of a rejuven-
ating process. But most of us, I suspect, would still identify with
a recent remark in a newspaper article that 'life after 40 is about
maintenance'.

So *is* there a middle-age, or mid-life, crisis, affecting every
aspect of our life, not least our working life? Or do we echo that
famous 1979 headline in the UK newspaper the *Sun*: 'Crisis?
What crisis?'[1]

Personally, I tend towards the latter. There is a charming story
by Tolstoy about a garden in which is buried a chest containing
the answer to all knowledge, and the secret of all wealth. Anyone
can come—the garden is not locked, there are signposts to the
area in which to dig, shovels are provided. But the one thing
treasure-seekers are warned is never, at any time during their
visit, to think of the big white rabbit which lives in the garden.
No one has ever yet found the treasure, because no one has been
able to resist picturing the forbidden image.

The power of imagination is overwhelming, and I have an idea
that many who believe they are experiencing a mid-life crisis are
doing so because their imagination has convinced them that they
are, or because someone else's imagination has convinced them
that they are.

It is possible to use our imagination another way, of course:
to motivate us to reach new heights, take on new challenges,
change our way of life; and I know of no better illustration of
this than one of the most enjoyable and heartening books I have
come across in recent years—*Tolstoy's Bicycle* by Jeremy Baker.
The title comes from the fact that Tolstoy decided, at the age of
67, to learn to ride a bicycle, and the book lists what men and
women through the centuries have achieved at every age from
−1 to well over 100; it contains such gems as the actress Dame
Edith Evans, still working at 78 and asking for her age to be
removed from the reference books as 'it may stop me getting
work', and George Bernard Shaw, planning at 42 for his funeral
procession to include oxen, sheep, poultry and an aquarium, their
purpose being to thank him for being a vegetarian ... It is a

marvellous antidote to the *awareness* of middle age, even if we don't feel we're in crisis.

Middle age itself is not the problem—it's our reaction to it. Hence the relevance of the passage about the Lion and the Unicorn, itself a good piece of imaginative writing and conjecture: Alice and the Unicorn think of each other as *monsters* until they meet and talk and understand each other better, leading the Unicorn to say finally: 'Well, now that we *have* seen each other . . . if you'll believe in me, I'll believe in you.' The same is true of mid-life crisis: it can appear a monster, until we get to understand what is meant by it, and then it seems not a crisis at all, but rather a figment of our imagination.

The Unicorn and the Lion also typify, perhaps, the two approaches to middle age, and any crisis associated with it: the former 'eager' and insouciant as regards threat, the latter 'tired and sleepy', wearily reacting to the change brought about by Alice's intrusion—though still capable of a spark of anger, perhaps out of frustration with his failing powers?

A SWOT analysis of what being middle-aged means illustrates these differences further:

The **strengths** of middle-aged people include maturity, discretion, experience, know-how and, usually, a well-developed network. Their **weaknesses** are fatigue, boredom, insecurity, clinging to the known (which may no longer be relevant), and, currently, an unwillingness to lobby to create a kind of *branding* of the middle-aged caucus, similar to that created by 'senior citizens' or the 'over 60s'—a highly organised and well-represented group, described by one organisation I know as 'grey panthers'. Their **opportunities** are openness to change, with an expectation of serendipity: after all, such people have plenty of intellectual assets—the question is how best to manage the portfolio. The **threats** to middle-aged people are those same assets: are they still useful, and do they enable going with the flow, or block it? As those I come across in my work tell me, people in their late 40s or 50s who find themselves looking for a job can have a tough time.

So how to maximise the strengths and opportunities, and minimise the weaknesses and threats, of those of a certain age? I would suggest six ways:

1   **Take advantage of your experience, and move steadily up the ladder.** Change is not always beneficial, and does not have to be cataclysmic—as those who work quietly to increase their knowledge and skill at work demonstrate. For these people it is their very stability and experience which are their main assets.

2   If the opportunity arises, **break out of your career rut.** It need not be as dramatic as the results of taking a certain brand of vodka or using a particular type of bath additive, but it may be—and Gauguin is a good example. But possibly Katherine Graham or even Queen Victoria are more appropriate models: the former, a legend in American journalism, took charge of the *Washington Post* when her husband committed suicide in 1963, and built up a powerhouse which toppled President Nixon; the latter, Empress of India, started learning Hindustani at the age of 68, to further her love affair with the sub-continent. The secret is to be like Charles Handy, who has just entered semi-retirement, but who still lives, he says, in constant expectation of doing something exciting and different—when he grows up.

3   **Put your personal insights at the service of wider concerns.** Diana Lamplugh used her anguish following the disappearance of her daughter Suzy to help others with similar experiences. Paul Eddington, a much-loved actor, gave a fine example of coping with crisis, wanting his epitaph to be 'He did very little harm'. Many older job candidates find personal (and some financial) satisfaction from investing their portfolio of experience in voluntary or charitable organisations which need it.

4   **Never give up.** At the age of 46 Gladstone was advised to give up politics because he was unpopular and lacking in judgement: he later became Chancellor, and Prime Minister

four times. Gitta Sereny, the author of the recent, much-acclaimed biography of Albert Speer, is in her 70s and started writing her book at the age of 60. Or take Senator Strom Thurmond, born 37 years after the American Civil War, who in 1996, at the age of 93, vowed to stand for an eighth term. It is still my experience that anyone, of almost any age, who really wants gainful employment, will be successful, provided they keep persevering and are flexible in their expectations.

5 **Don't leave youth.** I am not thinking here of modern Peter Pans like Sir Cliff Richard or Mick Jagger, who never seem to age, but rather of the healthy effect of spending time with younger people. Some do this permanently, by marrying partners much younger than they are, but just enjoying young people's company and learning from them can keep one's mind and outlook fresh. The youngest-looking middle-aged people I know will have nothing to do with holidays laid on by travel companies catering for the 'more mature', and are constantly looking for new experiences to share with the younger members of their family.

6 **Physically, fight nature.** I liked the advertising campaign by Levi Strauss in 1996 which used seasoned denim fans who were all over 60, giving a new zest and vigour to those who took part and new meaning to the phrase 'It's all in the jeans'. *Mens* (and womens!) *sana in corpore sano* is a good motto, and, as we saw in Chapter 24, there is little excuse these days for not keeping one's mind and body in trim. Even for those not in trim, there is still hope: there is the 'wonder drug', melatonin, a more palatable equivalent to drinking your own urine, and androderm, a kind of HRT for men of a certain age, applied to the skin as a patch. So far, though, there is no sign of a means to improve one's metabolism—it takes just a good, old-fashioned disciplined approach to exercise and dieting.

The poet Yeats wrote of 'reckless middle age', and it is a provocative and evocative phrase, conjuring up pictures of those who, with experience and wisdom behind them, put themselves at risk by thrusting forward eagerly to all that the future promises. The alternative picture comes from Alan Coren, in *Seems Like Old Times*: 'Middle is a dispiritingly practical age. There is a tendency to sift through unfulfilled dreams and begin chucking out the wilder ones.'

So, dispiriting mid-life crisis, or 'reckless' middle age?— as always, we have a choice. As for me, I prefer the latter, and like the optimism of the person who said, when she reached 100: 'If I'd known I was gonna live this long, I'd have taken better care of myself.'

Meanwhile, I am looking forward to my next visit to the dentist . . .

CHAPTER 27

Retiring by Nature

'Suppose we change the subject,' the March Hare interrupted, yawning. 'I'm getting tired of this. I vote the young lady tells us a story.'

'I'm afraid I don't know one,' said Alice, rather alarmed at the proposal.

'Then the Dormouse shall!' they both cried. 'Wake up, Dormouse!' And they pinched it on both sides at once.

The Dormouse slowly opened his eyes. 'I wasn't asleep,' he said in a hoarse, feeble voice: 'I heard every word you fellows were saying.'

'Tell us a story!' said the March Hare.

'Yes, please do!' pleaded Alice.

'And be quick about it,' added the Hatter, 'or you'll be asleep again before it's done.'

'Once upon a time there were three little sisters,' the Dormouse began in a great hurry; 'and their names were Elsie, Lacie and Tillie; and they lived at the bottom of a well—'

'What did they live on?' said Alice, who always took a great interest in questions of eating and drinking.

'They lived on treacle,' said the Dormouse, after thinking a minute or two.

'They couldn't have done that, you know,' Alice gently remarked; 'they'd have been ill.'

'So they were,' said the Dormouse; '*very* ill.' ...

'Why did they live at the bottom of a well?'

The Dormouse again took a minute or two to think about it, and then said, 'It was a treacle well.'

'There's no such thing!' Alice was beginning very angrily, but the Hatter and the March Hare went 'Sh! Sh!' and the Dormouse sulkily remarked 'If you can't be civil, you'd better finish the story for yourself.'

'No, please go on!' Alice said. 'I won't interrupt again. I dare say there may be *one*.'

'One, indeed!' said the Dormouse indignantly. However, he consented to go on. 'And so these three little sisters—they were learning to draw, you know—'

'What did they draw?' said Alice, quite forgetting her promise.

'Treacle,' said the Dormouse, without considering at all this time . . .

Alice did not wish to offend the Dormouse again, so she began very cautiously: 'But I don't understand. Where did they draw the treacle from?'

'You can draw water out of a water-well,' said the Hatter; 'so I should think you could draw treacle out of a treacle-well—eh, stupid?'

'But they were *in* the well,' Alice said to the Dormouse, not choosing to notice this last remark.

'Of course they were,' said the Dormouse; '—well in.'

This answer so confused poor Alice, that she let the Dormouse go on for some time without interrupting it.

'They were learning to draw,' the Dormouse went on, yawning and rubbing its eyes, for it was getting very sleepy; 'and they drew all manner of things—everything beginning with an M—'

'Why with an M?' said Alice.

'Why not?' said the March Hare.

Alice was silent.

The Dormouse had closed its eyes by this time, and was going off into a doze; but, on being pinched by the Hatter, it woke up again with a little shriek, and went on: '—that begins with an M, such as mouse-traps, and the moon, and memory, and muchness—you know you say things are "much of a muchness"—did you ever see such a thing as a drawing of a muchness?'

'Really, now you ask me,' said Alice, very much confused, 'I don't think—'

'Then you shouldn't talk,' said the Hatter.

This piece of rudeness was more than Alice could bear: she got up in great disgust, and walked off; the Dormouse fell asleep instantly, and neither of the others took the least notice of her going, though she looked back once or twice, half hoping they would call after her: the last time she saw them, they were trying to put the Dormouse into the teapot.

*   *   *

I suppose the Dormouse presents the archetypal picture people used to have of what retirement was like—a period of being semi-dormant, with the poor unfortunates who have just retired eager not to offend, but prickly if misunderstood or questioned (particularly by younger people); they are regarded as quaint, and two Zimmer frames short of an invalid car, and always at the mercy of the stronger or more dominant character. I find the parallel between the Dormouse being stuffed into the teapot, and elderly relatives being 'persuaded' to go into retirement homes, all too frightening.

How different is the reality today—at least for those who have made reasonable preparation for their retirement?

Mark and Evelyn were two of the participants on a pre-retirement course in which I was involved. I always enjoy these courses—there is a kind of 'end of term' atmosphere about them—and Mark and Evelyn were clearly looking forward to the holidays. They had been making financial preparation for some time, had started to plan how they were going to spend their leisure time and, as a vital part of their preparation, had bought a water bed—surfing the hairnet, perhaps?—and the humour was also far from dry. Dennis, on the other hand, looked worried and drawn: clearly retirement for him was not so much end of term as the start of a long term of a different kind, with no remission for good behaviour.

Their different reactions reminded me of the comment in Tom Stoppard's play *Indian Ink*, made by one of the English characters to her young Indian visitor about the British Raj: 'We were your Romans; we could have been your Vikings.'

For whatever our view of retirement, it is my experience that when that day comes when we have to leave for the last time our 'proper job' and enter the ranks of the 'grey panthers', it always comes as an invasion—never welcome but sometimes not as bad as we thought. And whether that invasion is seen as ultimately beneficial, like that of the Romans, or culturally harmful, like that of the Vikings, depends very much on the amount of preparation for retirement carried out in advance.

Not that preparation for retirement is new—enlightened companies have been providing it for years—but what *is* new is the context in which that preparation takes place, and the fact that individuals now realise the personal contribution they have to make to ensuring that their 'Third Age' is rewarding and fulfilling. To quote Allin Coleman, formerly director of the Centre for Health and Retirement Education at London University, and co-author of *Coping with Change*: 'The traditional image of retirement has gone forever. For present and future retirees, retirement means taking increasing responsibilities for themselves for managing one of life's major transitions.'

But present and future retirees include Mark, Evelyn and Dennis, so how are they, and others like them, going to manage this major transition?

● **Time:** First, unlike any other period of our life, we do not know how long our retirement will last. Childhood, education and adult working life, all have a comparatively fixed end time; but retirement can last one year, five years, twenty-five years—which makes planning for it, especially financial planning, more difficult. Second, just because estimating the length of time involved is so uncertain, the longer we take to plan and prepare the more we can take into account the variables and possibilities. In Chapter 25 I suggested a way of devising an ideal scenario for life by writing a paragraph each of ten basic life areas, describing your ideal scenario as you see it now. It should be capable of being realised within a reasonable time-span, and should be written in the present or perfect tense as if it has already happened—which unlocks your imagination and gives motivation. I recommend it again as an ideal way of looking—with a partner if you have one—

at how retirement might look to you, and the focus required to achieve it.

- **Finances:** There is now a wide variety of sources of advice on how to plan for different scenarios and new regulations are helping to ensure that the quality of that advice is usually high. Remember, though, that if such advice is free, it may be good but it will not be independent: if it is independent, it will not be free. Bear in mind also that retirement usually brings access to a large sum of money: it may be a compensatory award for taking early retirement, it may come from commuting part of a pension, or it may come from selling a house and moving. Nothing wrong with that, surely—but make sure that you act prudently by taking the best financial advice available to you, and thus provide the means of allowing you to enjoy your retirement for as long as it lasts.

- **Social:** Of course you need to handle your finances wisely, but remember that it is the *social* pressures which can make retirement a disaster, far more than the financial ones. Moving to the Costa Gaga for the sun and cheap living may seem a good idea, but how many people have soon fled back to *Neighbours*, rain and warm beer . . . and the friends they took for granted? So *think people*, and don't move away from your roots unless there are compelling reasons for doing so, and you can reasonably expect to replant them again in your new environment. Moving to be near your family is not necessarily such a reason—all too often younger families move with one or other partner's job, and then you could be really alone, without the benefit of grandchildren to torment and delight you.

- **Learning:** It is essential that you go on learning, broadening and sharpening your mind, and now is the time. Look at evening classes, day classes, the Open University, correspondence courses, residential courses, courses linked to holidays, courses on video or audio tape—the list is endless, and, if you are computer-literate and have access to a computer, the number of available courses, through the Internet or just through software, is increased a hundredfold. A friend of mine, now in his sixties, retired from a large computer company and now makes a reasonable income, with huge enjoyment for himself, creating on his computer backing tapes for choirs and soloists to learn their singing parts.

- **Interest:** My doctor tells me that if I want to die soon after retirement, I should work as hard as I can before 65, and then do nothing but relax. On the other hand, one of the happiest men I know, an ex-office manager, makes dolls' houses and Japanese min-looms, and converts French cartwheels into coffee tables, is busier than he was for his last three years at work, and his income is not bad either. It doesn't matter what you do—a sport, voluntary work, DIY, consultancy, a job (whether full-time or part-time)—but you must do *something*, and if you can't do it yet, use the time shortly before or after retirement finding out what you would like to do and learning the basics. There are so many opportunities, and if you are not sure about them, go to wherever locally you can get relevant advice—in the UK your local Citizens' Advice Bureau, your local library, or, for making contact with voluntary organisations, REACH in London: REACH stands for 'Retired Executives' Action Clearing House', though the word 'executive' is interpreted loosely, and it helps put people with certain skills, knowledge and experience in touch with organisations that need them. It is all summed up by the phrase everyone uses at different stages in life: 'One day, when I have the time or the opportunity, I'm going to . . .' Well now is the time, now is the opportunity—there won't be another.

- **The H factor:** I am talking about Health, Humour, Honesty and Hope: the first is obvious, but now is the time to ensure that as far as possible the body you have had for 50 years or so is good for another 30. Humour keeps everything in perspective, honesty provides the realistic framework for a totally new and challenging way of life—'I married him for better or worse, but not for lunch every day'—and hope, the last and only gift left in Pandora's box, remains when everything else looks disastrous or, perhaps worse, grey.

- **Mind-set:** Ultimately, preparation for retirement means coming to terms with its inevitability and the fact that it is ultimately down to individuals to learn how to make that third age of man a successful mixture of colour (with some chiaroscuro, of course), balance, perception and design, not a dissident daub on a wall. To quote Allin Coleman again: 'Learning is a life-long process. Along that journey how to retire presents one of the most challenging issues for the foreseeable future.'

Mark and Evelyn were learning to meet that challenge, or face that invasion, although they called it their 'voyage of discovery'—helped, of course, by that water bed.

CONCLUSION

Alice Grows Up
The future of work

. . . the egg only got larger and larger, and more and more human: when she had come within a few yards of it, she saw that it had eyes and a nose and mouth; and when she had come close to it, she saw clearly that it was HUMPTY DUMPTY himself. 'It can't be anybody else!' she said to herself. 'I'm as certain of it, as if his name were written all over his face.'

It might have been written a hundred times, easily, on that enormous face . . . she stood and softly repeated to herself:

> 'Humpty Dumpty sat on a wall:
> Humpty Dumpty had a great fall.
> All the King's horses and all the King's men
> Couldn't put Humpty Dumpty in his place again.'

. . . 'Don't you think you'd be safer down on the ground?' Alice went on, not with any idea of making another riddle, but simply in her good-natured anxiety for the queer creature. 'That wall is so *very* narrow!'

'What tremendously easy riddles you ask!' Humpty Dumpty growled out. 'Of course I don't think so! Why, if ever I *did* fall off—which there's no chance of—but if I did—' Here he pursed up his lips, and looked so solemn and grand that Alice could hardly help laughing. '*If I did fall*,' he went on, '*the King has promised me*—ah, you may turn pale, if you like! You didn't think I was going to say that, did you? *The King has promised me*—*with his very own mouth*—to—to—'

'To send all his horses and all his men,' Alice interrupted, rather unwisely.

'Now I declare that's too bad!' Humpty Dumpty cried, breaking into a sudden passion. 'You've been listening at doors—and behind trees—and down chimneys—or you couldn't have known it!'

'I haven't, indeed!' Alice said very gently. 'It's in a book.'

'Ah, well! They may write such things in a *book*,' Humpty Dumpty said in a calmer tone. 'That's what you call a History of England, that is.' . . .

'What a beautiful belt you've got on!' Alice suddenly remarked . . .

'It's a cravat, child, and a beautiful one, as you say. It's a present from the White King and Queen . . . They gave it me . . . for an un-birthday present.'

'I beg your pardon?' Alice said with a puzzled air . . . 'what *is* an un-birthday present?'

'A present given when it isn't your birthday, of course.'

Alice considered a little. 'I like birthday presents best,' she said at last.

'You don't know what you're talking about!' cried Humpty Dumpty . . . 'there are three hundred and sixty-four days when you might get un-birthday presents—'

'Certainly,' said Alice.

'And only *one* for birthday presents, you know.' . . .

Alice was too much puzzled to say anything, so after a minute Humpty Dumpty began again . . . 'Impenetrability! That's what *I* say!'

'Would you tell me, please,' said Alice, 'what that means?'

'Now you talk like a reasonable child,' said Humpty Dumpty, looking very much pleased. 'I meant by "impenetrability" that we've had enough of that subject, and it will be just as well if you'd mention what you mean to do next, as I suppose you don't intend to stop here all the rest of your life.'

*   *   *

Albert Einstein said, in an interview given in 1930: 'I never think of the future. It comes soon enough.'[1]

This book has attempted to explain how the Alice Principle is affecting the world of work today, and has tried to suggest ways in which individuals—and organisations—may respond to these changes in a positive way, to the benefit of all concerned.

'To be employed is to be at risk; to be employable is to be secure.' So what *will* it be like at work in the next century, if the trends mentioned in this book wend their way to the end? What it *won't* be like is this classic 'explanatory note' from the '80s:

> Regulation 3 of the Local Government (Allowances) Regulations 1974 ('the 1974 regulations') (S.I. 1974/447) made provision prescribing the amounts of attendance and financial loss allowances payable to members of local authorities. Regulation 3 of the Local Government Act (Allowances) (Amendment) Regulations 1981 substituted a new regulation for regulation 3 of the 1974 regulations. Regulation 3 of the Local Government (Allowances) (Amendments) Regulations 1982 ('the 1982 regulations') (S.I. 1982/125) further amends regulation 3 of the 1974 regulations, with effect from March 1982, by increasing the maximum rates of attendance and financial loss allowances. Regulation 7 of the 1982 regulations would have revoked both regulations 3 and 5 of the 1981 regulations (regulation 5 being a regulation revoking earlier spent regulations) with effect from 1ˢᵗ April 1982. These regulations preserve regulations 3 and 5 of the 1981 regulations by revoking regulation 7 of the 1982 regulations.

Yes—it was published near to 1984 . . .

Even in the most arcane areas of local government regulations, however, change has occurred, and there is some effort to improve communication and information flow so that ordinary people like you and me can start to understand what is going on.

So the future should at least be *clearer to understand* than the past has been, even though great uncertainties will remain.

I suggest there are four main areas of concern as we look into our crystal ball beyond the millennium (at the last turn of the century, they had the Crystal Palace . . .): Organisational Priorities; Contracts of Employment; Individual Issues; and Career Management.

ORGANISATIONAL PRIORITIES

There are, I believe, six areas in which successful organisations will be moving towards radical change from the incremental change we are now seeing:

1 The concentration on decentralisation will move towards an obsession with innovation, as all concerned with an enterprise will be empowered to look for new solutions, new processes, new opportunities for growth.

2 That very empowerment will itself move towards a passion for serving customers, as organisations focus on the clients, the markets, and differentiation by offering customer satisfaction.

3 The disintegration typical in some sectors and companies, caused by rapid technological, social and global change, will settle down into more routine changes in organisational design.

4 (Business Process) Re-engineering, the cause of much fundamental change in both organisations and individuals, will lead to a constant resistance to conformity, as new ways of doing *everything* are sought. To try to resist this resistance will be like trying to nail jelly to the wall.

5 'Learning', in a formal, or even an informal, sense will give way to an upsurge in curiosity: it will be the difference between an outside activity imposed, suggested or encouraged by the 'learning organisation', and a natural, innate seeking after knowledge and self-development.

6 The focus of Total Quality Management will shift from the negative reduction of things that go wrong to the positive encouragement and growth of things that go right. This will

be true for processes as well as people: Ken Blanchard's phrase from *The One-Minute Manager*, 'Catch them doing something right', will still be relevant.

CONTRACTS OF EMPLOYMENT

There have been, and will be, interesting developments in the relationship between the organisation and the employee, the continuance of trends going back to the '80s:

The contract 1984

Individual offers	*Organisation offers*
Loyalty	Security
Reliability	Progression (grade and pay)
Conformity	Status
Functional skills	Training and development (?)

The contract 1994

Individual offers	*Organisation offers*
Flexibility and specific skill	A job, today
Performance and accountability	Cha(os)
	(nge)
	(llenge)
Long hours	More money

The contract—2004

Individual offers	*Organisation offers*
Learning	Employability (internal/ external)
Knowing how to learn	Flexibility of contract
Clear value-added	Opportunity for reputation
Commitment	Rewards for achievements

There is therefore a clear trend shifting responsibility for career development, self-development, away from the organisation towards the individual, and a loosening of the contract regarding reward towards flexibility, mobility and transferability.

INDIVIDUAL ISSUES

- **Core!** In view of the new structures in organisations, with smaller cores and an increase in ancillary, or peripheral, service providers, the individual employee will need to decide where he or she will invest time and talents. The choice will be whether to be, and stay, part of the core, with possible burn-out in his or her 40s, or whether to develop within the niche markets and companies, which will change constantly like an amoeba. The answer will have something to do, I suspect, with the individual's choice of lifestyle.
- **Flatter structures** will lead to fewer opportunities for promotion, so individual motivation will have to come from other factors, such as learning opportunities, job enrichment and creative reward schemes. Pay, as Herzberg found, is a neutral factor here.
- **Fairy godmothers** will have gone, if they ever existed. Responsibility for career development will mainly fall on the individual.
- **Bite-sized chunks** will typify career progression, rather than a steady pilgrimage with one organisation over forty years. Networking and constant retraining to maintain employability will be essential to ensure fewer and shorter gaps between the chunks.

CAREER MANAGEMENT

Taking responsibility for the past will involve three imperatives:

- **Recognise the significance of the past:** you are the product of all that has gone into making you what and who you are; build on that, don't regard it as irrelevant, and take with you into the future the nuggets that will make you wealthy, in career success terms.
- **Understand the reality of the present:** things have changed and will go on changing; burying your head in the sand, in paperwork or in nostalgia (though as someone said, that isn't what it used to be), is no answer. But then you don't really think it is, do you, or you wouldn't be reading this book?
- **Take responsibility for the future:** use all your talents to prepare for the niche opportunities of the future. Charles Handy told a friend of mine how he once found himself sitting next to a woman on a 'plane to Boston, Massachusetts. He discovered she was a nurse, who specialised in looking after families in which the mother had given birth to twins, triplets or more. When Handy asked if she was busy in this highly specialised area of nursing, she replied that she couldn't cope with demand: the cause was fundamentally future-orientated, and explains why, as I mentioned in Chapter 1, it is reckoned that half the jobs in the US in the year 2000 do not yet exist. Boston has a high proportion of professional couples, who tend to plan their families; when they do decide to have a family the incidence of multiple births in women who come off the pill after a long period is higher than average—and hence this nurse's new, and highly successful, occupation. That is taking responsibility for the future . . .

A FINAL WORD ON SURVIVAL

If, after all that has gone before in this book, I were asked to give some fundamental advice on how to survive and grow in the work climate of the next ten years, I would offer six areas on which to concentrate:

- **Welcome change and risk:** you can only resist change, accept it, or welcome it. Try to be one of those who is known for his or her enthusiasm in welcoming change, and in being prepared to consider risk as a necessary corollary to change.
- **Festina lente:** the Latin tag, meaning 'make haste slowly', is necessary also as a modifying influence on your willingness to accept change. I have seen too many companies rush into re-engineering, make severe cuts to the workforce, and then, six months later, have to take back some of those same people because the cuts went too deep, and they have lost valuable staff resources—and know-how. I have seen individuals rush down obvious blind alleys in their search for future success. Enthusiasm, yes. But wisdom even more so.
- **Learn the business:** it's no use burying yourself in the IT or Training departments any more, telling yourself that what 'the business' gets up to is no concern of yours. Everyone now has to understand what the business is about, where it's going and above all what his or her place in it is likely to be.
- **Sort out your support systems:** nobody at work now is an island, so make sure you are part of an effective team and that you have your network in place (which you carefully review), so that you are aware of what is going on and can call on others to help you when you are under pressure. And remember it is a mutual process.
- **Go on learning:** never stop. Francis Bacon said that knowledge is power, and never has that been truer than now. What is more, there are far more opportunities to learn, and to use that learning, than ever before.

- **Regard every job as a project:** the days of settled, long-term careers with one company are over: it is time to readjust to the new demands, pack your knapsack and head for London, or wherever *your* streets are paved with gold.

I suppose one could conclude that the future will be an exciting time, with warm echoes of the past; as Alan Bennett has said: 'I've always felt that the past was over and that somehow I'd missed it. Now it's starting all over again.'[2] I suppose one could add that it will be a time of great surprises, with plenty of 'unbirthday presents' to carry one along.

But Humpty Dumpty should have the last word, as one book ends and another . . . well, that must be *your* story:

. . . we've had enough of that subject, and it will be just as well if you'd mention what you mean to do next, as I suppose you don't intend to stop here all the rest of your life.

How to Make a Victorian Carpenter's Hat

The carpenter's paper hat was a badge of profession—it showed to everybody that you *were* a carpenter. It was used during the nineteenth century, and is perfectly drawn by Tenniel in the drawing above.

In the steps that follow, be careful to ensure that edges, folds and angles are as straight and true as you can make them.

1 Take a single sheet from the *Financial Times* or equivalent (the measurements are approximately 39 × 60 cms). This is the size of a Victorian broadsheet, and gives the best results. There are single sheets in the FT—otherwise cut a double page in two.

2 Fold a diagonal to make a square (the FT gives one of 41 cms).

3 Cut off the extra piece of paper.

4 Unfold the square and fold the other diagonal.

5   Unfold the square again and fold into two halves: crease well only for 10 cms or so in from each outer edge.

You should now have folds radiating at 45° angles, making a star shape.

6   Fold each corner in turn into the centre point. Unfold the square.

7   Fold the corners again, but this time to the farther fold which you created in step 6, beyond the centre point. Unfold the square. THE CENTRE FOUR SQUARES ARE NOW THE TOP OF THE HAT—YOU MAY WANT TO MARK THEM TO HELP YOU LATER.

8   Fold the corners again to the fold created in step 7. Cut off these triangles—if you are using the FT the long side of the triangle is 22 mm long. You should be left with a square with the corners cut off.

9   Turn the sheet over, and fold one of the longer edges (where you cut off the triangles) to the nearest fold (about 1 cm away). Fold it again on to itself to make a double fold. Repeat this step with the three remaining long edges. This double fold will become the rim of the hat, holding it together.

10 Now comes the difficult part: take one of the diagonal folds that would have gone to each corner of the square had these not been cut off. Unfold the rim to the right of this diagonal, and then fold the diagonal fold to the right into this unfolded area. Fold the other diagonal adjacent to the unravelled rim to the left into this same area. This will generate two triangular flaps that fold in and 'point' to each other: these are the sides of the hat. This is tricky, because one of the folds running vertically to the edge of the sheet must be reversed to achieve this.

11 Fold the unfolded rim back up so that part of it stands above the other folded rims, and tuck this flap over the other side rims to hold it all in position.

12 Finally, repeat the process on the other side to complete the
    hat.

You have now made a carpenter's hat. Imagine doing this with
a sharp knife on the kitchen table each day before going out to
work. Like traditional carpentry, it uses ratios to get it all to
work, not measurement as we tend to do today.

And that's not a bad parable for successful management today,
which calls for instinct and sensitivity as well as knowledge and
sheer technique.

Chapter Notes

Chapter 3
1 Quoted from the *Tao te Ching* of Lao-Tse. See Bibliography.
2 For details of Scott Adams' books of Dilbert cartoons, see Bibliography.
3 Bennis has written extensively on leadership: see Bibliography.
4 For the full article by Gore Vidal, see *The Listener*, 7 August, 1975.
5 Sydney Carter's celebrated song can be found in *One Hundred Hymns for Today*, published by Hymns Ancient and Modern.

Chapter 4
1 This summary of Warren Bennis' views is a synthesis of the ideas discussed in his various books. See Bibliography.
2 See Bibliography for John Kotter's various books on leadership, especially *Force for Change: How Leadership Differs from Management*.
3 See Bibliography for one publication by Tom Peters, one of the most widely read American management gurus of our time.

Chapter 5
1 The survey of human resources practices in the retail financial services sector was produced in 1992 by KPMG Management Consulting. Write to Robin Linnecar, KPMG Career Consulting Ltd, 20 Farringdon Street, London, England EC4A 4PP.

Chapter 7
1 Meredith Belbin's books on Team Roles are listed in the Bibliography.

2 For details of Geoff Cooke's views, see his book *Skilful Rugby Union* (details in Bibliography).

Chapter 8
1 The Cyril Connolly quotation comes from his *The Condemned Playground: Told in Gath*, and is taken from *The Oxford Book of Humorous Quotations* – see Bibliography.

Chapter 9
1 The report by Linda Holbeche, 'Career Development in Flatter Structures', can be obtained from Roffey Park Management Institute, Forest Road, Horsham, West Sussex, England RH12 4TD.

Chapter 11
1 This letter from John Radford, Professor Emeritus of the University of East London, appeared in *The Times* of 22 December, 1994.
2 The IPD paper 'People Make the Difference' may be obtained from the Institute of Personnel and Development, 35 Camp Road, London, England SW19 4UX. Tel: 0181-971-9000.

Chapter 14
1 *The Economist*, vol. 335, no. 7918, 10 June, 1995.

Chapter 15
1 From an interview between Charles Handy and one of the partners of KPMG Career Consulting for their publication *Career Matters*, Summer 1993. Copies may be obtained from KPMG Career Consulting Ltd, 20 Farringdon Street, London, England EC4A 4PP.

Chapter 16
1 From a speech given in February 1964. Quoted in *The Oxford Dictionary of Humorous Quotations* (see Bibliography).

Chapter 19
1 Benjamin Franklin, *Poor Richard's Almanac* (1758).

Chapter 21
1 The Personnel Standards Lead Body document, 'A Perspective in Personnel', may be obtained from the Employment Occupational Standards Council, 2 Savoy Court, Strand, London, England WC2R 0EZ. Tel: 0171-240-7474.

Chapter 22
1 The quotation by Saki comes from *The Square Egg* (1924): 'Clovis on the Alleged Romance of Business'.

Chapter 23
1 For the text of the Monty Phython series, see Bibliography.

Chapter 24
1 The quotation from G. K. Chesterton comes from his *What's Wrong with the World*, Part 4: Folly and Female Education.
2 Alan Coren, *Seems like Old Times* (1989) – see Bibliography.

Chapter 26
1 The *Sun* headline of 11 January, 1979 summarised Prime Minister James Callaghan's remarks of the previous day: 'I don't think other people in the world would share the view [that] there is mounting chaos.'

Conclusion
1 From a 1930 interview on the 'Belgenland', quoted in *The Oxford Dictionary of Humorous Quotations* – see Bibliography.
2 From *Enjoy* (1980), quoted in *The Oxford Dictionary of Humorous Quotations* – see Bibliography.

Bibliography

Adams, Scott (1995). *Dilbert: Bring Me the Head of Willy the Mailboy!*, London: Boxtree.

Adams, Scott (1996). *Dilbert: It's Obvious You Won't Survive by your Wits Alone*, London: Boxtree.

Arnold, Roseanne (1994). *Roseanne: My Lives*, London: Century.

Atherton, John (1992). *Christianity and the Market: Christian Social Thought for our Times*, London: SPCK.

Baker, Jeremy (1995). *Tolstoy's Bicycle: Who Did What When*, Oxford: Helicon.

Barr, Lee and Barr, Norma (1989). *The Leadership Equation: Leadership, Management and the Myers-Briggs*, Austin, Texas: Eakin Press.

Belbin, R. M. (1996). *Team Roles at Work*, 2nd ed., London: Butterworth-Heinemann.

Belbin, R. M. (1996). *Management Teams: Why They Succeed or Fail*, London: Butterworth-Heinemann.

Bennis, Warren G. (1992). *On Becoming a Leader*, London: Business Books.

Bennis, Warren G. *On Becoming a Leader*, read by the author. 2 cassettes, 120 min. London: Simon & Schuster Audio.

Bennis, Warren G. and Nanus, Burt (1986). *Leaders: Strategies for Taking Charges*, New York: Harper & Row.

Bennis, Warren G. and Townsend, Robert (1996). *Reinventing Leadership: Strategies to Empower the Organisation*, London: Piatkus Books.

Bennis, Warren G. and Townsend, Robert. *Reinventing Leadership: Strategies to Empower the Organisation*, read by the authors. 2 cassettes, 120 min. London: Simon & Schuster Audio.

Blanchard, Kenneth H. and Johnson, Spencer (1984). *The One-Minute Manager*, London: Fontana.

Blanchard, Kenneth H. and Johnson, Spencer. *The One-Minute Manager*, 1 cassette, 60 min. London: Simon & Schuster Audio.

Blanchard, Kenneth H. and Lorber, Robert (1985). *Putting the One-Minute Manager to Work*, London: Fontana.

Blanchard, Kenneth H. and Lorber, Robert (1987). *Leadership and the One-Minute Manager*, London: Fontana.

Brearley, Mike (1985). *The Art of Captaincy*, London: Hodder & Stoughton.

Bridges, William (1996). *Jobshift: How to Prosper in a Workplace without Jobs*, London: Brealey Publishing.

Bunyan, John (1678). *Pilgrim's Progress*, paperback ed. 1970, Harmondsworth: Penguin.

Coleman, Allin and Chiva, Anthony (1991). *Coping with Change: Focus on Retirement*, London: Health Education Authority.

Cooke, Geoff (1991). *Skilful Rugby Union*, London: A. & C. Black.

Coren, Alan (1989). *Seems Like Old Times*, London: Robson Books.

Coren, Alan (1990). *More Like Old Times*, London: Robson Books.

Covey, Stephen R. (1992). *Seven Habits of Highly Effective People: Powerful Lessons in Personal Change*, London: Simon & Schuster.

Covey, Stephen R. *Seven Habits of Highly Effective People: Powerful Lessons in Personal Change*, read by the author. 1 cassette, 90 min. London: Simon & Schuster Audio.

Deming, W. Edwards (1988). *Out of the Crisis: Quality, Productivity and Competitive Position*, Cambridge: Cambridge University Press.

Deming, W. Edwards (1990). *Sample Designs in Business Research*, Chichester, Sussex: John Wiley & Sons.

Fiennes, Ranulph (1994). *Mind Over Matter: His Epic Crossing of the Antarctic Continent*, London: Mandarin.

Fiennes, Ranulph. *Mind Over Matter: His Epic Crossing of the Antarctic Continent*, read by the author, 6 cassettes. Bath: Chivers Audio Books.

Handy, Charles B. (1995). *The Empty Raincoat: Making Sense of the Future*, London: Arrow Books.

Handy, Charles B. (1996). *Beyond Certainty: The Changing World of Organisations*, London: Arrow Books.

Harvey-Jones, John (1994). *Making it Happen: Reflections on Leadership*, London: HarperCollins.

Herriot, Peter and Pemberton, Carole (1995). *New Deals: Revolution in Managerial Careers*, Chichester: Sussex: John Wiley & Sons.

Howe, Geoffrey (1995). *Conflict of Loyalty*, London: Pan Books.

Kanter, Rosabeth Moss (1992). *The Change Masters: Corporate Entrepreneurs at Work*, London: Routledge.

Kanter, Rosabeth Moss (1992). *When Giants Learn to Dance: Managing the Challenges of Strategy, Management and Careers in the 1990s*, London: Routledge.

Kotter, John P. (1988). *The Leadership Factor*, New York: Collier Macmillan.

Kotter, John P. (1990). *Force for Change: How Leadership Differs from Management*, New York: Free Press.

Kotter, John P. (1995). *New Rules: How to Succeed in Today's Post-corporate World*, New York: Free Press.

Lao-Tse: *Millennium Series* (1994). Grail Acres Publishing Co.

Mayhew, Kevin (1984). *Hymns Old & New*, Bury St Edmunds, Suffolk: Kevin Mayhew.

Montgomery, Cynthia A. and Porter, Michael E. (1991). *Strategy: Seeking and Securing Competitive Advantage*, Cambridge, MA: Harvard Business School.

The Monty Python Team (1990). *The Complete Monty Python*, London: Mandarin.

Mortimer, John (1983). *Clinging to the Wreckage*, Harmondsworth: Penguin.

Obeng, Eddie and Crainer, Stuart (1995). *Making Re-engineering Happen*, London: Pitman.

One Hundred Hymns for Today (1982). Norwich: Hymns Ancient & Modern.

Partington, Angela (ed.) (1994). *The Concise Oxford Dictionary of Quotations*, Oxford: Oxford University Press.

Partington, Angela (ed.) (1996). *The Oxford Dictionary of Quotations*, Oxford: Oxford University Press.

Pease, Allan and Cox, Peter (1992). *Body Language: How to Read Others' Thoughts by Their Gestures*, London: Sheldon Press.

Peters, Thomas J. (1994). *The Tom Peters Seminar*, London: Macmillan. Petronius Arbiter (1936). *Works*, Loeb Class. Lib, translated from Latin by W. H. D. Rouse, Cambridge, MA: Harvard University Press.

Porter, Michael E. (1990). *The Competitive Advantage of Nations*, London: Macmillan.

Scott, Martin (1993). *Time Management, Sunday Times* Business Skills Series, London: Century Business.

Sherrin, Ned (ed.) (1966). *The Oxford Dictionary of Humorous Quotations*, Oxford: Oxford University Press.

Spark, Muriel (1969). *The Prime of Miss Jean Brodie*, Harmondsworth: Penguin Books.

Spark, Muriel and McEwan, Geraldine. *The Prime of Miss Jean Brodie*, read by Geraldine McEwan. 2 cassettes, 180 min. London: HarperCollins Audio.

Tory, Peter (1993). *Giles: A Life in Cartoons: the Authorised Biography of Britain's Leading Cartoonist*, London: Headline.

Twain, Mark (1969). *Pudd'nhead Wilson*, Harmondsworth: Penguin Books.

Waugh, Evelyn (1989). *The Ordeal of Gilbert Pinfold*, London: Penguin Books.

Williams, Stephen (1994). *Managing Pressure for Peak Performance*, London: Kogan Page.

Yate, Martin John (1991). *Great Answers to Tough Interview Questions*, 1 cassette, 45 min. abridged with booklet. London: Kogan Page.

Yate, Martin John (1992). *Great Answers to Tough Questions*, London: Kogan Page.

Index